MW01170628

A Broken Girl

Kiki Ellyse

Copyright © 2024 by Kiki Ellyse

All rights reserved.

No part of this publication may be reproduced, distributed, or transmitted in any form or by any means, including photocopying, recording, or other electronic or mechanical methods, without the prior written permission of the publisher, except as permitted by U.S. copyright law. For permission requests, contact Kiki Ellyse.

The story, all names, characters, and incidents portrayed in this production are fictitious. No identification with actual persons (living or deceased), places, buildings, and products are intended or should be inferred.

ACKNOWLEDGEMENTS

Firstly, I would like to thank God for everything that he has done for me so far and in the future. Now, I would like to thank my family, friends, my book sisters, and church family for encouraging me to keep writing and finishing this book. I want to send a very special thank you to my editor, Tabitha Sharpe. Thank you so much for taking my story in and helping it come to life. This book was eleven years in the making, and it's finally here. The story that you are about to read is completely fiction but based on a true, real-life story. I have always dreamed of being an author, and now it has come true. I really hope you enjoy my characters and their journey as I did when I wrote this book. I really, really hope that you all will continue to be on this writing journey with me because this is only the beginning.

Table of Contents

Kiki Ellyse

Chapter One

"Starr, come down! It's time to eat!"

I sighed. I was so close to finishing up my room, and it's taken me two days to do this, but I'd finish putting up my clothes before I went downstairs.

I'm Starr Brown and I just moved from Compton, CA to Birmingham, AL. I live with my parents, Darren and Sierra Brown, my eleven-year-old sister, Skylar, and my two-year-old little brother, Sekani.

My momma was born and raised in Birmingham, then she went to Alabama A&T University, where she met my daddy on campus. From what they told me, it was love at first sight when they met through mutual friends, and the rest was history. They dated all four years, they joined a fraternity and sorority in the same year, became the "It" couple in the Alabama A&T University, both graduated the same year, got married, and moved to Los Angeles for a new beginning.

My daddy is a banker at Regions Bank, and my mom is a registered nurse. Even though we stayed in Compton, we had a very nice house. Daddy found a better banking job in Birmingham, and that was one of the reasons why we moved here.

I liked the city. It wasn't very fast paced or as lit as LA, but I liked the southern hospitality, and the wings were sooooo good.

Just as I thought about the wings, I came to the dining room and realized that we had wings and fries for dinner. I was happy because I smelled my favorite flavor so far: hot lemon pepper wing with Cajun ranch fries and a Keke Pooh, which is like Kool-Aid but much better. I was recommended this by my cousin.

"Hey, Starr," my momma smiled at me as she finished setting up the table. "Nice to see you out of your room today."

"I was still unpacking."

"And how's that going?"

"It's going well. I'm almost done."

"That's good."

At that moment, the front door opened and closed, and my daddy walked into the living room.

"Hola, mi familia," Daddy said as he kissed my momma and kissed my forehead.

"Where's the other two knuckleheads?"

"Right here, Daddy," Skylar told him as she held Sekani.

"Oh, there you are, I was wondering why it's so quiet."

"Sam, leave my babies alone," Momma chimed in.

"What do you mean? I helped make them."

"But I was the one who carried them for nine months."

"Because you wanted kids, so I've given them to you. Be careful what you ask for."

Momma playfully smacked Daddy on his arm.

I chuckled.

"OK, break it up. We're starving."

We sat around the table, and we began praying for the blessings of the food.

"Amen," we all said.

"Amen!" Sekani shouted, making us all laugh.

We began to eat our wings, and I was in heaven. I'm sorry, but Birmingham wings couldn't touch LA's wings. I can't describe it, but it was something that you had to try to understand.

"So, Starr, we got some news," Momma announced.

I stopped eating and perked up.

"So, we decided to enroll you to Avondale so you can be with Kay-Kay."

I clapped and squealed. Kayla, AKA Kay-Kay, was my first cousin/best friend. My only friend, actually. We had been close ever since we were tots. Even though we were miles away from each other, every time we visited each other, we never skipped a beat. When she found out that we were moving to Birmingham, she was ecstatic. I wasn't even there yet, and she had all kinds of different plans for us. Matter of fact, I was meeting up with her tomorrow, and we were supposed to go bowling with one of her friends.

"We figure it best for you to be in a school where you know somebody and won't lead you astray," Momma said.

"Yeah. Because we don't need a repeat of what happened back in Cali," Daddy expressed.

Absolutely not.

***

I finally finished unpacking my stuff and I finally got the chance to rest. Then, I heard a knock on the door.

"Come in!"

My momma came in and sat on my bed.

"I see that you finished unpacking," Momma noticed.

"Yeah, I did."

"How are you feeling?"

"I feel good."

"No, I mean, how do you feel about everything? Like, moving from home to here?"

I took a deep breath. "I feel fine. This was much needed after everything that happened."

"Yeah, I agree. Are you excited about your new school?"

"Yeah, especially now since I'll be going with Kay-Kay."

"Yeah, I know that, but you gotta realize that she has her own friends and probably won't be around you all the time. So, you're going to have to try to make friends."

Oh God.

The thought of me making friends was enough to make me ill. No seriously, it would make me physically sick. When I was eleven years old, I was diagnosed with Social Anxiety Disorder. Which made sense because when I was younger, I was too afraid to talk to anyone. I couldn't walk up to anyone and talk to them because it would make me break down and cry. It was really bad back then before my parents took me to therapy. Once I started cognitive behavioral therapy, it helped me learn how to carry conversations, how to journal, how to calm myself down through breathing techniques, how to stop negative thoughts and think positively, and how to have self-confidence. It was working for a while, and I even gained a friend. Then something happened that pushed me backwards to where I lost a friend and my confidence. I hadn't been to therapy since.

"Baby, I know this will be difficult for you, but I know that you are capable of making some good friends. You're funny, nice, and sweet. Anyone would be happy to be your friend. Maybe a cute boy might take notice of you."

I rolled my eyes at the thought of me talking to boys after what happened.

"Momma, that's not gonna happen."

"You'll never know."

"You know Daddy will cut up if he sees me with a boy."

"Don't worry about your daddy. I'll handle him. Just be Starr, OK?"

"OK?"

She kissed my forehead as she exited my room.

I leaned back in my bed and let out a sigh.

This was really my new life.

***

4

It was a beautiful day. My parents were at work, my siblings were at my grandparents' house, and I was on my way to Kay-Kay's house to go bowling. The walk wasn't bad. It would take me ten minutes to get there.

As I was walking, I looked around and admired the neighborhood. It was a suburb with nice houses, with nice green front yards. It was way different from LA. I was shocked because I expected it to either be in the country because it was the south or be in the war zone because of the latest shootings. Don't get me wrong, there had been shootings, but not much from the area I lived in. I lived in a neighborhood called Avondale on the south side of Birmingham near the University of Alabama in Birmingham also known as UAB. Avondale was known for the restaurants, small antique stores, and being diverse. But, so far, I liked Birmingham.

I was getting close to Kay-Kay's house, and when I turned the corner, I saw three girls coming down the streets. All of them were brown-skinned, wearing the latest clothing, and they were very pretty. Especially the one in the middle. She looked like the "It" girl in the black teen movies. I guessed they were from around here. Even though I was scared, I should try to speak to them and try to make friends.

They're getting close.
Girl, say something to them.
I don't know if I can do it.
Yes, you can. Just do it. You never know.
I don't know...
Here they come. It's now or never.

As they were going to walk past me, I swallowed my pride, took a deep breath, smiled towards them, and said, "Hey!"

The girl in the middle gave a stink face, and the other two girls just burst out laughing as they kept walking.

Well, that didn't work.

After feeling embraced, I just started to fast walk to Kay-Kay's house and frantically knocked on her door.

"Who is it?" the familiar voice asked behind the door.

I playfully rolled my eyes.

"Who do you think it is?"

I heard a squeal, the door unlocked, opened, and there was one of my favorite people in the world.

"Starr!" Kay-Kay jumped and squealed.

"Kay-Kay!" I exclaimed as I gave her a big hug.

"How are you, cousin?" she asked as we let go of each other.

"I've been great. How about you?"

"I'm great now that you're here. Now, I got someone else to mess with."

We both laughed because she was the only child, and I was the sister that she always wanted.

"What about your friends?" I asked.

"Ehh… I can only annoy them to certain extents. But now I got you here, I know who I can go to before I fight someone."

I laughed. "You're crazy, you know that?"

"Been telling people that for years, but they keep messing with me, Starr."

"Why not walk away?"

"I've tried. Multiple times. They just keep coming at me, and I want to punch somebody."

Kay-Kay was always the type to fight, and I was the one who tried to keep the peace.

"Nobody held you back?"

"Oh, we have. Multiple times," voice said behind us. Coming down the stairs was a gorgeous, brown-skinned girl with a short, pixie hair.

"Starr, this is Lauren, my other best friend. Lauren, this is my cousin/other bestie, Starr."

"Hey! Nice to meet you, I'm Lauren."

Breathe Starr, and just say Hi.

6

"Hey, I'm Starr."

"Nice to meet you."

I nodded my head.

"But yeah, people be trying me, cousin," Kay-Kay said.

"Yeah, but sometimes you'll escalate the situation," Lauren added.

"I don't."

Lauren gave her a look.

"Most of the time, I don't."

"Mm-hmm."

I chuckled a bit as I kept listening to their conversation. Lauren seemed like a nice person. I just hoped she liked me.

"So, Starr, I heard you're from LA."

I nodded my head.

"Birmingham is way different than what you're used to, huh?"

"Yeah." I nodded.

"You must be shy?"

"Oh, yeah, very shy," Kay-Kay chimed in. "But, once she warms up to you, she's actually pretty cool."

"OK, that's fine. I completely understand."

I let out a sigh of relief in my head. I made Kay-Kay promise not to say anything to anyone about me having social anxiety because I didn't want a repeat of what happened back in LA.

"So, y'all ready to bowl?" Lauren asked.

"Yeah, I haven't bowled in a minute," I replied.

"Me either," Kay-Kay answered. "I can't wait to beat y'all."

"Oh, please," Lauren scoffed.

"Wow, I haven't been here for a while, and you already talkin' smack," I joked.

"It's what I do, and y'all still love me."

"Oh, whatever." I chuckled.

"What time is your dad going to pick us up?" Lauren asked Kay-Kay.

"When he gets off work, and he gets off at six."

I looked at the time on my phone, and it was 5:06 PM.

"That gives us time to chill for a bit. Y'all want to listen to some music?"

"Yeah, what you got?" Lauren asked.

"We can listen to K'Won's new song."

My ears and eyes perked up. K'Won was the hottest teen rapper out right now. He won multiple music awards and was nominated for two Grammys for Best New Artist and Best Rap Performance. He mainly rapped about his life growing up, making money, and how to treat a girl right.

"Oh my God, he is my favorite rapper," I blurted out.

"Oh my God, mines too," Lauren said to me.

"Yeah, that is one fine man," Kay-Kay giggled.

"Kay-Kay, that man is sixteen," Lauren replied.

"So, he's close to being eighteen, so he's close to being a man."

"Girl, just play the music."

Kay-Kay connected her phone to the Bluetooth and played K'Won's new hit, *Turn The Bass Up*. It was about him riding around in a car with his friends, the car blasting music, having fun, and not caring about what people had to say.

We were all rapping the lyrics together and having fun. We rapped a few more of his songs before we left to go bowling. We did three games, and we each won one game. We all enjoyed each other. I got to know Lauren and she seemed like a genuine, sweet person. I could tell she liked me. Now, I was looking forward to what was ahead.

Chapter Two

I was woken up by the alarm from my phone. I groaned because I knew it was time for me to get up for school, and honestly, I didn't want to go, even though I said that I wanted to go the other day. But I knew if I didn't get up, my mom would let Skylar jump on my bed to get me up. After five minutes, I got up, did my hygiene, got dressed, and went downstairs.

"Hey, everyone," I said to everyone at the dining room table, which was my daddy, Ashley, Sekani, and my momma.

"Hey, Starr!" everyone said in unison.

I swear sometimes I hate when they do that.

"Really?" I jokingly asked.

"Yep," my dad said and laughed.

"I like your outfit, Starr," my mom said as she observed my attire.

I looked down and said, "It's nothing, it's just simple." All I was wearing was a denim jacket top with a white tank top, black tights, and a pair of white Adidas shoes. I was also rocking a twenty-inch straight black sew in.

"Well, it looks good to me," Momma said as I sat down at the table to eat the eggs, bacon, and pancakes that my momma made. After we were done eating, we gathered all our things and said bye to Daddy so we could go. Daddy went to his car to go to his job, and Skylar, Sekani, and I went to Momma's car.

We pulled up at her new middle school to drop off Skylar.

"OK, Skylar, have a good first day," Momma said to her.

"I hope so," Skylar said nervously from the back seat.

Skylar had always been a social butterfly and made tons of friends back at home. But now, she had to start all over again, and she was nervous about this new journey in her life.

"You'll be great, Skylar," I said to her, encouraging her.

She smiled at us, kissed Sekani from his car seat, and left the car heading to the front doors of the school as Momma pulled off.

After we dropped off Sekani at his daycare, we pulled up in front of my new high school, Avondale High School and I let out a huge sigh of nervousness and anxiety. I looked at the school, and it was big but not as big as my old high school. I could tell this was a predominantly black populated school because all I saw were beautiful black kids of all shades and sizes. That made me extra nervous because of how the kids were dressed in trending name brand clothing, the freshest pair of Jordans, and the cutest weaves, braids, and wigs. *How can I compete with that? How can I keep up with the trends with these down south people?*

"Starr, I know that look. Look at me." I did as I was told. "I know this is new to you, and I know that you had difficulties with school back at home, but this is your chance to start over and make friends and new memories. **Luke 11:9-10** 'So I say to you: Ask and it will be given to you; seek and you will find; knock and the door will be opened to you.' 'For everyone who asks receives; the one who seeks finds; and to the one who knocks, the door will be opened," I said at the same time as her.

"There you go!" She kissed my forehead, and I grabbed my bookbag as I got out of the car.

"Have a good day, Starr'," Momma said as I was going to close the door.

"Momma!" I said to her while looking around to see if anyone heard her.

"I'm sorry, Starr. I love you."

"I love you, too."

"Have a good day."

"Yeah, I hope so, too," I said to myself as I closed the car door and walked towards the branch that was by the side of the front door to wait for Kay-Kay. As I waited, I looked around and checked out the students. It was like being in a black movie. I heard YoungBoy and Moneybagg Yo blasting from cars. I saw black boys smiling with grillz, a couple of kids doing TikToks, girls yelling with their friends, and cars with big wheels. But at least these kids seemed a little calmer than kids in my old high school. My old high school back in Compton, McNair High School, was very rowdy and ratchet. There was always drama going on with the students, fights every two weeks, shootings at the football teams, even teachers would get into it with each other. Maybe stuff like that happened here, too, but let's hope not. I felt a buzz in my bookbag and realized it was my phone. I pulled it out, and I saw a text message from Kay-Kay saying:

Cuzzo/Bestie: WYA

Me: I'm in the front of the school sitting on the bench.

After I sent the text, I looked up, and I saw the same group of girls from the other day. The middle girl looked fly, but her other two friends looked plain. That let me know she was the queen bee. She rocked a white, long-sleeved top, a blue, short skirt, with a pair of blue and white Nike shoes. She also had long, straight weave that reached down to her butt. All the boys were looking at her, whistle-calling her, saying,

"Dang, who's that?"

"Aye, lil' mama!"

"Hey, what's your number?"

I could tell that she just loved the attention. She had confidence, beauty, and made heads turn when she stepped into the room. As for me, I had no doubt that I had a pretty face, but I never had a boyfriend, had never been on a date, and I never had a boy come and talk to me back at home. My social anxiety was one of the reasons I didn't really go out to out-of-school functions like parties, sporting events, or going to concerts, nor did I have any friends to go with. Now this was probably my chance to change that and finally make some friends and be social.

I felt a buzz from my phone, and it was another text from Kay-Kay saying:

Kay-Kay 🖤 : Look at the door.

I turned my head toward the door, and I saw Kay-Kay and Lauren standing at the door. I laughed as I got up from the bench with my bookbag and headed to the door towards the girls hoping to leave my past life back in Compton and to begin a new chapter at my new school.

We walked into the school, and I was baffled at how big the hallways were. My old school's hallway was so small and narrow, it would take at least ten minutes to get to your locker. But here, I could actually feel a breeze in the hallways. As we were walking, there was a white boy running in the hall.

Wait, there's a white boy in this school? Of course, it's some white kids here. It's Avondale. It's a whole bunch of white kids here. It shouldn't come as a shocker to you because McNair had black, white, Latinos, even some Asians. So, you're used to having white classmates.

I realized he was running towards us and stopped right in front of us.

"Matt, what's wrong with you? Why are you running in the hallway this early?" Lauren asked.

Mark might be white, but he had drip like a black person.

Mark had sandy, brown curly hair, a black and red Vlone shirt, skinny blue jeans, and a pair of Air Jordan 11 Retro Breds. He even had a sparkling watch and a chain on his neck. He was cute even though I wasn't really into white boys.

Mark breathed hard as he turned toward Lauren and said, "Lauren.... Blue...is here...at...the...school."

Lauren widened her eyes and said, "What? How is he back from alternative school already?"

"I... don't know."

Mark looked and pointed towards me and asked, "Who is this?"

Kay-Kay stepped up and said, "This is my cousin, Starr, she's from LA. Starr, this is one of our friends, Mark Jefferson."

Mark reached his hand out to shake mine, and I reached back.

"Nice to meet you," he said.

"You too."

"Now we got the introductions out of the way," Lauren said. "Why didn't anybody text me to give me a heads up?"

"I didn't find out until now," Kay-Kay said to her.

"I just saw him in the hallway a few minutes ago," Mark said.

I jumped into the conversation, "I don't know who Blue is."

"My bad," Kay-Kay said to me. "Blue is the school's main bad boy. Always getting in trouble or fighting."

"OK. So, what's the big deal? Did he do something to you guys?"

"No, he just has had a huge crush on Lauren since middle school, and she is avoiding him."

I couldn't help but laugh. I mean, she was a very pretty girl. At least she knew that someone thought she was pretty.

"But, I'm not interested," Lauren said.

"Cap, but OK," Kay-Kay said.

"Anyway, we got to go. We need to go to the auditorium to get our schedule before the bell rings."

"OK, well it's nice to meet you," Mark said to me.

I replied saying, "You too."

We walked to the auditorium, and we went to the lines with our last names to get our class schedule. Few minutes later, I got my schedule and I waited for Kay-Kay and

Lauren at the door. As I waited, I took a look at my class schedule.

English 101- 8:30-9:20 am (Hmm… Interesting.)
Algebra I 9:30-10:50 am (Ugh, I hate Math.)
Study Hall/ Lunch- 11:00am-1:00
Biology 1:10-2:00 pm
Theater-2:10-3:30 pm (Ohhhhhhhhhhhhh)

That wasn't bad beside the Math part. I could chill, study, do homework, and even sleep. I could also…

"Dang, baby, what your name is?" a guy said who was standing in front of me. He had to be at least 6'0, brown skin, a white tank top, black skinny jeans, and black and gold Foams. He had chains around his neck and tattoos on his arm. He looked like he could be sixteen or seventeen or probably older. I looked around to see if he was talking to someone else.

"I'm talking to you, ma," he tells me,

"I'm not your ma. I have a name," I said to him. My momma taught me that no boy should approach me calling me shawty or lil' mama because that would have boys thinking that you were easy to impress and could try to manipulate you.

He threw his hands up defensively. "My fault, my fault. Can you please tell me your name?"

I was kind of hesitant at first, but because it was my first day at a new school, and I didn't want to be called the stuck up, new girl.

"Starr, I said.

"OK, Miss Starr," the boy said. "My name is D-Rod."

I nearly laughed when he said that. *D-Rod. What kind of nickname is that?*

"Where you from? Because you are definitely not from around here." D-Rod asked me.

"Compton."

"OK, OK, that's cool."

Don't get me wrong he was fine, but there was something about him that seemed off.

RIIIIIINNNNGGGG.

I looked around, seeing that everyone was walking to their classes. I realized that the bell finally rang. Thank God.

I turned to him and said, "Umm, I'm sorry I have to go."

"Whoa, whoa, whoa," he said to stop me. "Let me get your number first."

Kay-Kay popped up in between us with her back facing me and said, "I don't think she wants to talk to you, D-Rod."

Thank God, again.

She pulled me down the hall to the stairwell with Lauren following behind us.

"I'll see you around, Miss Starr!" D-Rod yelled as we walked away. I looked back at him, and he winked at me. It was like he expected me to turn around when he called my name. I turned back to Kay-Kay, who let go of my arm as we walked up the crowded stairwell, and I asked her, "Girl, who was that?"

"Destin Cole," Kay-Kay answered, "but he prefers to be called D-Rod."

"How old is he?"

"He's sixteen and in the 11th grade," Lauren said as we made it to the second floor. "He's cute and all, but he's a player, so be careful around him."

I scoffed, saying, "Trust me, I'm chilling. I don't have time for boys right now."

At least, not right now.

***

We finally reached our first class, English 201. I felt nervous because I didn't know what this school year would hold, but I hoped I could make it out OK. I found a seat in the middle part of the class, and Kay-Kay sat next to me on the left and Lauren sat in front of me.

I was sitting there taking deep breaths and shaking my leg to calm me down because I was just so anxious.

"Are you OK?" Kay-Kay asked after noticing that I was nervous.

"I'm fine," I said to her "Why you ask?"

"Because you seem shaken up. Did D-Rod say something to you that made you scared?"

"No, he didn't. Just feeling nervous about this school year. You know… after everything."

"Don't be. As long as you don't start drama or mess, you will be alright." I laughed a little bit as a black boy and another white boy walked in.

"Hey TJ, hey Jake."

"Hey, Lauren," Jake said.

"Yo, Lauren," the black boy said. "I seen your boyfriend coming down the hall."

"Shut up, TJ," Lauren said. "He is not my boyfriend."

Lauren grabbed her hoodie and put it on to hide her face while holding her head down. The boys started laughing as they took their seats.

"Lauren, why wouldn't you give my man a chance?" TJ asked.

"I'll give 13 reasons why."

He laughed at the reference to the Netflix TV show.

"That's a good one, but for real, what's wrong with him?"

"He brutally beat a guy up last year and went to alternative school because of it."

The white boy put his finger up in objection and said, "Umm... to be fair, that guy was a senior who was trying to fight him, and when Blue tried to walk away, the guy pushed him hard."

"Well, why did he want to fight him?" Kay-Kay asked.

"Because the guy's girlfriend was being too friendly with him," TJ said.

"Wasn't she a senior, too?" Kay-Kay asked.

"Yep, a senior talking to a freshman."

"That's creepy, though."

"It is," Jake said before he turned to me. "I haven't seen you around."

"No," Kay-Kay said before I did. "This is my cousin, Starr. She's here from California."

They both looked shocked.

"Why would y'all move to Birmingham?" TJ asked.

"My dad has a new job in the Region building for IT."

"OK, that makes sense. Well, I'm TJ, and this white boy is Jake."

"So, what does TJ mean?"

"Terrence Royce Jr.," they all said.

"Thank you for that unnecessary introduction," TJ said as he looked annoyed.

"Anytime, Bud," Jake joked.

"Well, it's nice to meet you," I said. "So, do y'all have any tips for me for this school?"

"Well, it's a couple," Lauren spoke up. "Don't talk to these upperclassmen. They're always looking for freshmen to prey on."

"Don't be hanging out with the potheads because they are always in a hospital for whatever reason," Jake said.

"Stay to yourself, and don't start anything because these girls are ready to fight. Especially about boys in this school," Kay-Kay said.

"Don't talk to anyone on the football or basketball teams. They always have different girlfriends every week," TJ said.

Kay-Kay looked at him confused and asked, "Ain't you and Jake on the football team?"

"Ummmm…yeah."

It was a momentary pause between all of us.

"I guess you knew that firsthand."

All of us were laughing, and when I turned to the door, another boy came in, and I almost died for a moment because of what I saw. Right in the doorway was the finest boy I had ever seen in my life since Michael B. Jordan. He was a caramel-skinned guy with some of the most beautiful locs.

He came in and sat two rows across from me. I swear he was like a boy who just stepped out of my dreams. He was just so perfect.

I turned to Kay-Kay and whispered, "Girl, who is that?"

Kay-Kay saw who I was talking about and said, "Oh, that's JaQuan. Popular, really smart, and a hooper."

Ooooohhh… a triple threat.

He looked at me, and I quickly turned. *Why am I hyping myself up? I can't even go talk to him, and I doubt he will come to me. But I can daydream though.*

Then, I was snapped back into reality when the pretty middle girl and her crew came in. *I don't know her like that, but I can tell whenever she's in the room, she always funks up the mood in the room.*

"Hey, JaQuan," the middle girl said.

"Wassup, Ary?"

Ary? So, that's her name? Are they dating? Are they talking? No, no, no. We're not together. Who knows? They might be friends. Hopefully.

Kay-Kay scoffed, "I was hoping she wouldn't be in any of my classes."

"Who is she?" I asked her.

"Aryanna Black. She's the meanest girl in the school. She's Avondale High's version of Regina George."

Oh, great. A mean girl.

"And her Karen and Gretchen are Katrina, with the ginger hair, and Rayanna, with the long braids," Lauren added.

"Don't be around them, though," Kay-Kay warned me. "They are literally snakes in a pond."

I shook my head. *You don't have to tell me twice.*

A moment later, an older man, probably no older than thirty, walked in the classroom. I knew he was our teacher because everyone that was standing up immediately sat down.

"Good morning, scholars."

"Good morning," we all responded.

He suddenly got up, went out of the classroom, and closed the door. We were all confused until he came back in.

"Let's try this again. Good morning, scholars!"

"Good morning!" We sounded so much better.

"OK, I'm just trying to make sure I'm in the right classroom. My name is Mr. Wright. I will be your English teacher for this school year. Now, I hope all of you are Sophomores because if you're not then you and your mama need your butt whooped." We all busted out laughing.

"Like I said, I am Mr. Wright. I am a Morehouse graduate, I have worked here for at least seven years, and fun fact—I love to cook."

"You're gonna cook for us one day?" TJ asked.

"Well, we'll see when you get an A. How about that?"

"Aww man, that means you have to work twice as hard so we can have a good meal," Jack said as we all laughed.

"OK, since I've told you a little about me, now I want to know a little bit about you guys. I want to know your name, your favorite hobby, the last book you've read, and a fun fact about you. Let's start row by row."

I hated introductions. I had to force myself to get up and tell people who wouldn't hang out with me my name and my information. I didn't know what to say to these people, and I didn't have a fun fact besides me being a big fan of K'Won.

Then it was my imaginary future man's turn.

"My name is JaQuan Watts." *JaQuan Watts.* "My favorite hobby is playing basketball, the last book I read was the Will Smith autobiography, and I'm the only sophomore on the varsity basketball team."

"OK, I see you," Mr. Wright said. "You gonna bring in a championship this year?"

"I'm gonna try."

"Alright man, that's what I like to hear."

Then it was Aryanna's turn. It took her a minute before she even said anything.

"Well," she said before popping her tongue. "Y'all know me as Aryanna. My favorite hobby is having fun, and I like to be on Facebook." She sounded nonchalant and like she didn't care. I looked over at Kay-Kay, and she looked at me and shook her head.

Mr. Wright cleared his throat. "Well, Ms. Aryanna, you forgot to say, 'My name is...' and your last name."

She looked up at him. "They know who I is," she said snapped.

"They know who I *am*. Looks like you need this class more than I thought."

Everyone was ooh-ing except her. She gave the "if staring at someone will kill you" type of look at Mr. Wright. TJ turned to us and said, "She's mean but can't speak correct English."

A few of us, including me, snickered a bit with TJ. Although it was funny, I tried to stop myself because I didn't want to bring any attention to me. It didn't work.

"What's funny?" Aryanna asked as she looked at me.

I immediately stopped and looked down at the desk.

"OK, next person," Mr. Wright said as he tried to de-escalate the situation.

As they continued down the rows, I could've sworn that I heard her mumbling to her friends saying, "I should just smack her."

Now, the moment I dreaded. It was my turn.

I looked around the classroom and all these kids were staring at me. This was why I hated the first day of school. I didn't like people to know who I was because I might have a panic attack just by hearing my name in the hallway. Not to mention that I didn't want Aryanna to know my name. But now, I didn't have a choice. Oh no. The thoughts were coming back again.

What if I stutter again?
What if I mess up?
What if they laugh at me?
What if JaQuan doesn't like me from my introduction?
Oh God, here we go again.
Breathe.
Remember what Dr. Bailey said.
Eye contact.

"Um, my name is Starr Brown. My favorite hobby is reading books, the last book I read was "Love Radio," and a fun fact about me is that I moved here from Los Angeles."

"Seriously?" I nearly had a heart attack when Mr. Wright yelled.

"I'm from LA, too. What part?"

"Oh, uhh, Compton."

He might be from Santa Monica or Beverly Hills.

"Oh OK! I'm from Leland."

"Really?" *Yes! Someone I can relate to about LA stuff.* "I'm from downtown."

"That's great. I'm glad I met another Angeleno."

As he moved to the next person on my row, I couldn't help but to smile. I conquered another fear in the past two days! I was so happy! Kay-Kay and Lauren even looked at me to give me a thumbs up for doing a great job. I looked forward, and I noticed that JaQuan was looking back at me, smiling. I wanted to wave at him, but I couldn't, I just couldn't. He slowly turned around in his seat. I wished I could wave to him to at least to get some interaction. But, right now, I didn't care. I smiled the whole class because I did the impossible. Normally, this would be painful for me to do this, and I would just flat out refuse to do it. But I conquered it.

After everyone introduced themselves, Mr. Wright went over what we would be doing for the school year. We would be reading a story in our literature book, which included Shakespeare, Edgar Allen Poe, and Mark Twain. *Boring...*

But we would be looking into African American literature, too, which included James Baldwin, Langton Hughes, Alice Walker, and many others. *Fun!* We would have to do a weekly quiz about the story every Thursday, and every Friday, one or two students would do a presentation based on a theme of the story we read that week. It could be a mini play, a song, a poem, a speech, etc. That terrified me. It was bad enough that I had to introduce myself in front of a whole classroom from my desk, but in the front of the classroom? I would die.

Finally, the bell rang, and it was time for us to go to the next class period. I got up and headed to the hallway to wait for Kay-Kay and Lauren. When I saw JaQuan walk by, I paused. He looked at me as he walked past me, and he smiled at me.

Is he smiling at me because I was in his way, and he was trying to be nice?

Or does he like me?

I smiled back admiring his beauty as he walked away. I got snapped back to reality when I got a hard bump in the shoulders. I nearly fell to the ground when I looked up and saw it was Aryanna and her crew.

"You don't know how to say excuse me?" she said to me as I stood up. I was petrified. I didn't want confrontation. Not again.

"Is there an issue here?" Kay-Kay said as she came to me.

"Better tell your friend to watch where she's going," she said as she walked away.

"Guh, you better gone somewhere." Kay-Kay turned back to me. "Are you OK?"

I nodded my head yes even though I was lying. I could tell that was only the beginning of a long school year.

Chapter Three

I finally made it to my Algebra class. This was my only class without Kay-Kay and Lauren, and I was nervous. I found an empty seat in the front because I wasn't good at Math and for me to be able to pay attention to the lesson.

A few minutes later, TJ and Jake walked into the classroom. I was happy because there were some people in the classroom that I somewhat knew. They saw me and started walking towards me.

Oh God, here they come.

Is my breath alright?

What should I say to them?

What if I gave a wrong impression?

Starr, breathe.

"Hey, Starr, right?" Jake asked as he sat beside me.

Look him in the eyes. I turned to him and said, "Yeah. Hey."

Oh my God, that was dry and not welcoming.

"You like Math, Starr?" TJ asked me as he was sitting behind Jake.

"No," I said quickly. "Matter of fact, I hate math."

"What a coincidence. We suck at math, too."

I laughed at his honesty.

Then, Jake said, "Yeah, so don't ask us anything about any equations, because nine times out of ten, we're not going to know the answer."

"Looks like I have to pay attention in class for the three of us, huh?" I asked, hoping that it was funny.

They both chuckled as TJ said, "Yeah, sounds like you might have to."

Hey, I'm funny!

But then I thought about it.

"Wait a minute, don't think I'm the only who's gonna work."

"Well, why not?"

"Because I'm gonna struggle, too. So, how can I help you when I'm struggling too?"

Starr, here your smart mouth goes again.

"Yeah, you're right about that."

Am I right? Yeah, I'm right.

"Looks like we all got to help each other," Jake said.

"As long I pass this class."

Another milestone! I was able to make conversation and have a small disagreement with someone and won! I wish I could call Dr. Tatum and let her know my progress.

***

The bell rang for one of the things I dreaded the most: lunchtime. That was the most social time for high schoolers. Where the athletes could talk about sports and talk trash. Where the girls gossiped and talked about their crushes and how their looks glowed up over the summer. Where anime watchers debated who was the better fighter. Where the smart kids talked about their future and what college they wanted to go to. For most people, this was the best part of the day. For me, this was the most terrifying part of high school besides gym. For one, because of my social anxiety. For two, I didn't have any friends back home so I would usually eat by myself.

There would be times where I'd be hiding in the bathroom and stay there until there were about a good thirty minutes left in lunch just to avoid contact as much as possible. I wanted to do better by being there on time, but old habits die hard. I hid for ten minutes before I got the courage to go to the lunchroom.

Come on, Star, it's a new school year at a new school. You don't want to come off as weird.

I made it to the door of the cafeteria, and before I opened it, my head was full of thoughts.

What if I do something to embarrass myself today?

What if I—

No, no, no. We're not going to over think and have a panic attack.

Breathe.

I opened the door and there were so many people. All I could feel were eyes on me. All the voices suddenly decreased for a moment, and I just felt overwhelmed. I just wanted to turn around and go back to the bathroom, but I pushed through to the line.

Luckily, besides the lunch lady asking what I wanted, no one tried to talk to me. But my biggest problem was finding a place to sit.

After looking for two minutes, I found Kay-Kay waving me over to the table she was at. At the table were Kay-Kay, Lauren, and two other girls. The closer I was, the more I noticed that the two girls were twins. *That's so cool!* I knew some twins back at h—

Boom!

I felt a huge bump on my shoulder that nearly made me fall and almost drop my lunch. I looked up, and I saw it was Aryanna.

"I thought I told you to watch where you're going," she said to me as I sat up.

"I-I-I'm sorry," I said.

Why did I stutter?

"Yo-yo- you- you'll be sorry, alright."

"What's the issue, Aryanna?" Kay-Kay came behind me.

"She bumped into me twice."

Umm, no. You bumped into me twice. On purpose.

But instead, I said, "It was an accident."

"How would you like it if I accidentally knock you out?"

I was about to have a panic attack. This was why I didn't want to come to lunch; to avoid this type of situation.

"You gonna have to fight me," Kay-Kay steps to her.

"No, no, no," I heard a male voice behind me, and I turned to see it was JaQuan. He was so fine up close. "We're not finna fight on the first day of school."

"Well, tell your friend to stop messing with my cousin," Kay-Kay said.

"Well, tell your cousin to watch where she is going next time."

"OK, OK, OK," JaQuan said as he jumped in. He turned to Aryanna. "It's the first day of school, and we are trying to have a good day without drama. Can we just let it go?"

Aryanna looked at me for a good minute before she replied, "'Ight, 'Quan. I'll let it go just because you told me to. Y- Y-you better watch yourself." She turned to walk out of the lunchroom. I literally stood there about to vomit because I knew she was about to make my new school life here hell.

I thought I could escape this type of situation, but it followed me here.

"Thanks, JaQuan," Kay-Kay said.

"You're welcome."

I turned away and walked to our table without thanking him. Not that he did anything wrong, but I was scared to talk to him, and I was really shaken up.

"Are you OK, Starr?" Lauren asked as I sat at the table.

"I'm fine." *I'm not fine. My anxiety is through the roof right now.*

"Starr," Kay-Kay said as she sat back down. "Why didn't you say thank you to JaQuan? He was gonna ask you if you were OK."

I felt bad because he did help diffuse the situation, and now he'd think I was weird and wouldn't talk to me. But I was used to being the weird or awkward girl, so I was fine with that.

"I'm sorry. I was just a little shaken, that's all."

"Don't let Aryanna round you up like that," one of the twins said.

"Yeah, she'll get over it," the other twin said. "I'm Ashley."

"I'm Amber."

"Hi, I'm Starr."

"Nice to meet you," Amber said.

"Not to be rude, but how can I tell you apart?"

I hope I didn't offend them.

"It's OK, you'll tell us apart based on our personality and attitudes," Amber said.

"OK, I'll remember that."

We all sat, eat, and talked for the next twenty minutes. I learned the twins were singers hoping to be famous, and if not, then they would be nurses. The bell ringing meant lunch was over. I wanted to hurry back to the study hall and try to avoid Aryanna as much as I could for the rest of the day.

***

Finally, I made it to my last class of the day: Theater. I didn't know much about theater besides *Rent* and *Hamilton*. I had no interest in acting—I preferred to be behind the scenes. Our classroom was actually the auditorium. It was big, and it kinda reminded me of the auditorium on *High School Musical.*

I saw the twins, Amber and Ashley talking to Mark. I went over to them and sat next to them.

"Hey, Starr," Mark said as I sat down.

"Hey, Starr," the twins greeted in unison.

"Hey, guys," I said. "Whew, last class."

"Yes, Lord," Amber said. "It's only the first day, and I'm already over school."

Mark then said, "Man, Amber it's just the first day of school. It can't be that bad."

"Bruh, two girls in my Health class were about to fight because they were beefing on Facebook all summer long."

Jesus.

"Wait. What? Why would they wait until the first day of school to fight? Why not during the summer just to get it over with?"

"Your guess is as good as mine."

I'm flabbergasted. On the first day? I had to ask, "What were they fighting about to begin with?"

"It started over a boy, who, by the way, has a girlfriend. Apparently, they both found out that they were talking to the same boy and got into an argument. But, once they found out that he has a girl, they called a truce. Their mutual friend decided to be messy and went back and forth with both of them, telling them what one supposedly said about the other. Now after a few weeks of throwing shade on Facebook, they decided they want to confront each other in class on the first day of school."

"And that's why I can't be a F-boy," a voice said behind us. We turned, and it was a tall, caramel-skinned guy with a blue Polo shirt and black pants.

"Hey!" Mark and the twin said as they stood up.

"What up, Mark?" the boy said as they man-hugged.

"Nothing much, Ty. It's good seeing you, man."

"Good to see you, too. What up, twins?"

"Hey, Ty," they said in unison as they hugged him.

He saw me looking at him, and I turned my head.

Oh, God. What if he comes up to me and yells at me for looking at him? I can't take another confrontation.

He walked to me and leaned towards me.

Breathe.

"Hey, I'm Ty. What's your name?"

I'm shocked.

"Oh. Um, Starr."

"Nice to meet you, Starr."

"That's Kay-Kay's cousin," Amber said.

28

"Oh, yeah, Kay-Kay did tell me about you. So, you're straight outta Compton, huh?"

I laughed at the NWA reference. "Yeah, you can say that."

"Just know I'm a goof, so don't mind me."

"I think I have an idea."

We all jumped when we heard loud clapping sounds as a woman wearing colorful hippie clothes with long locs walked on the stage and said, "All right, class, how are we doing?"

"Good!"

"OK, I'll be taking the roll, and I'll go over what we're gonna be doing this school year."

As she was taking the roll, I turned to the twins and asked, "Have you taken her before?"

"I haven't, but Amber has," Ashley said.

"She's not bad," Amber said. "She's actually fun. I had her last year for choir. She's cool."

"I hope so."

"OK, class," the teacher said. "My name is Ms. Bailey, and I will be your Theater teacher for the school year. In this class, all of your grades will be graded on attendance and participation, That's it. Quick easy A, am I right?"

The students agreed.

"Good, now, we will play some games. Is that OK?"

"Yeah!" the whole class replied.

"OK! Let's get started."

***

Kay-Kay: Meet me in front of the school so we can walk home together.

Me: OK, I'm coming.

The dismissal bell rang, and it was the end of my first day of being in a new school. I was walking through a crowd of students in the hallway, and I'm terrified. I didn't like to walk through a crowd because I thought people were talking about the new girl.

Who is this new girl?

Where does she come from?

Why she—

No, NO! Starr, take a deep breath and bre—

Out of nowhere, I felt a push behind me, and I fell.

Oh, no, no, no, no, no, no, no. This is my worst fear.

I looked up and saw Aryanna and her friends laughing at me.

"Oh, I'm s-s-s-sorry. Are yo-ou-ou OK?" Aryanna laughed as her friends laughed.

"Aryanna…" I looked up, and Ty was pulling me up. "I saw what you did. You need to apologize."

"She was in my way. I don't have to apologize." She rolled her eyes as she and her friends walked away, laughing.

"You OK?" I shook my head saying yes even though I was still shaken up.

"Do you want me to walk you to where you need to be?"

"No," I quickly said. "I'll be alright."

"OK, be careful."

I just started walking away. I just wanted to get away from   this   school. I made it outside, safely that is.

I reached the bus stop to where I found Lauren, Kay-Kay, and the twins.

"What up, cuz?" Kay-Kay said as I approached them. *Please God, don't let them notice something.*

"Y'aaaalllll," Lauren said.

"What?" everyone else said.

"Did y'all hear about Selena and Karlee almost getting into a fight in Mrs. German's class?"

"Baaabbyy…" Amber was ready to spill the tea. "I was in that class, and when I tell you that fight was a whole mess…"

"What led up to that fight?"

"Girl, all I know is that Vic went back and forth with both of them for the entire summer, and one of his homeboys snitched on him to Selena during lunch."

"Which homeboy?" Amber asked.

"Tashaun."

"See! I knew he was fake," Ashley said. "But continue."

"So, basically, Selena went up to him asking where Vic was. He then said something along the lines of 'I don't know. Last time I seen him, he was by Karlee's locker.'"

"Oooooo!" they all exclaimed.

"Selena put two and two together. She saw Karlee in our class, and it went down."

"Didn't they fight over him before?" Amber asked.

"Yes! Do you remember when...."

As their conversation continued, I saw Aryanna and her crew walking passed us, and she was just looking at me like she wanted to fight me, but she laughed and kept walking. *Why is she just laughing? Was she trying to see if we were going to do something?*

"Starr," Kay-Kay said, interrupting my thoughts. "You straight?"

"Yeah, I'm good." I lied.

"OK, because the bus is here." I looked up and there was a big, yellow bus right in front of me.

"Oh, my bad." I chuckled, and I got on the bus.

I'm so ready to go home and try again tomorrow.

Chapter Four

This past week was the greatest and most difficult first week of school I'd ever had. I'd started to open up more to my new friends. I loved my new teachers, especially Mr. Wright and Ms. Bailey. They were the perfect example of Black Teachers Matter. Mr. Wright had us having real discussions about topics related to the short stories we were reading. We would have a good conversation and have heated debates, and it was fun.

In Ms. Bailey's class, she had us do improv skits and had us do acting exercises. As much as I didn't want to act, her classes and exercises were so much fun.

But on the other hand, this week was bad for me because of Aryanna. As if Monday wasn't bad enough, the last three days were torture. On Tuesday, she put gum on my hair, and it got stuck until I noticed it until the end of school. On Wednesday, my book bag went missing in Mr. Wright's class, and it "magically" ended up at Mark's desk. Mark swore up and down to Mr. Wright that he didn't take my book bag. The thing is, I knew it wasn't him. Mr. Wright asked me if I knew anyone who would take my book bag, and I shook my head saying no, knowing there was a name in the back of my mind. Then, there was Thursday. "Someone" took my backpack again, and we were looking all day for that, and we had to go to the principal to try to figure out who took it. We ended up finding it in the trash can after school.

I didn't tell my parents about this because I absolutely didn't want my mom and dad to make a big deal about it. I was used to this.

It was finally Friday, and I was so ready for the weekend so I could regroup and take a breath.

I walked in the lunchroom for lunch feeling good because they were serving my favorite food, pizza. I grabbed my lunch tray and went to the table where Lauren, Kay-Kay, the twins, and Mark were sitting.

"Hey, guys," I said as I came up to the table.

"Hey!" everyone said.

As I sat down at the table, I heard a voice. "Mind if I sit here?" I looked up, and it was a very handsome guy. He kind of reminded me of Damson Idris.

"Uh, yeah, we do mind, Blue," Lauren said.

Oooohhh, so this is Blue.

"Come on, Lauren, I'm trying to come and eat with y'all."

"Are you trying to eat with us, or are you trying to eat with Lauren?" Amber asked.

"Maybe both," Blue answered.

"It's not going to happen, Blue," Lauren said.

"Why not?"

"Because I'm a straight A student and a good girl. You're a bad boy. What would you need with a good girl?"

"Sometimes, a bad boy needs a good girl to make him settle down."

"Oooouuuuuuuu," everyone at the table said.

"Oh, y'all mind your business," Lauren fussed at us.

We all broke out laughing.

"Look, I won't hold you up, but don't believe what everyone is saying about me. Everything is not what it seems." Blue gave her a wink and walked away.

"Man, Lauren, why won't you give my boy a chance?" Mark asked.

"Man, look, mind your business."

"He seems nice," I said. "That's because you don't know him like we do. We grew up with him, and he is very prone to violence."

"But, to be real, Lauren," Kay-Kay jumped in, "most of the fights that he was in were instigated."

"Yeah," Ashley said. "Remember when he got into a fight with Cedric?"

Lauren looked at her. "You mean the time he ended up in the hospital?"

"Hey, he did talk about his dead granddad."

Lauren's eyes darted at Ashley. "So, that excuses him from sending someone to the hospital?"

"No. But you don't know what really happened between them."

"So, what happened?"

"You just have to ask him."

Lauren groaned and put her head on the table.

"Hey, at least you have someone who shows interest in you," Kay-Kay said, "We're all over here single and lonely with no one showing interest."

"I won't say that," Mark jumped in. "I heard someone got an eye on Starr."

I quickly turned to him and said, "Me?"

"Who?" the rest of the girls exclaimed.

"I can't tell you that. Just know that he said he will come up to talk to you soon."

"Uhhhh," I groaned in annoyance. "Can't you just give me a hint please?"

"Nope. Might give my boy away."

"So lame," Lauren said.

"He made me swear not to tell."

"I bet it's D-Rod," Ashley jumped in.

Everyone at the table started saying, "Nahhhhhh."

Mark threw his hands up and said, "Y'all know I don't talk to him."

"Yeah, that's a hard no for me," Kay-Kay said. The rest of the girls shook their heads in agreement.

D-Rod had been trying to talk to me this past week, but I'd been making excuses to leave, and whenever I was with my friends, they would block him, and we just walked away. From what the girls were telling me, he was a known gang member in the neighborhood and would occasionally sell drugs. That was a pass for me. I knew so many male classmates that were killed or would go to jail because of the streets of Compton. I just couldn't be around that.

"I wouldn't want to be with him anyway," I said.

"Girl, good," Lauren said. "Because I don't need to be in jail for hurting anybody. So, if you see him in the hallway and he comes towards you, you better be a track star and run."

I chuckled a bit.

The twin blurred out, *"She's a runner, she's a track star,"* We all followed in with the lyrics, but we stopped when something fell on my plate and splashed everywhere. I froze with my hands up with my mouth open. I looked down, and there was an open bottle of milk that was still leaking, and the milk was all over my food, and all over my clothes. All I could do was gasp and try to breathe. As I got up and looked to my right, I saw Aryanna and her friends just laughing.

"Oh, m-m-m-my bad, S-s-s-Starr," Aryanna taunted, "I-I-I didn't see you."

Amber got up and yelled, "Ay, bruh, you did that on purpose!"

Kay-Kay stood up. "Man, if I wasn't on the dance team, I would…"

The words were fading from my mind because I noticed people were looking at me. Probably talking about me. Probably laughing at me. I was now breathing hard.

Oh no, not again.

I can't deal with this again.

I can't take the laughing.

I have to go.

I just ran out of the lunchroom and sprinted to the restroom and into the stall. I started breathing hard like I couldn't breathe. I could hear the door open and a voice saying, "Starr, you in here?" I could tell it was Lauren.

"Starr," I heard Kay-Kay's voice now. "I know what you're doing. Just breathe."

I did as she told me. I was starting to calm down. But my nerves were shot.

I looked up at the stall, and someone was handing me some extra clothes.

Lauren said, "I know that they probably not fly to you, but it's better than having wet, soaked clothes for the rest of the day."

I looked, but I didn't know what she was talking about. She handed me a very cute white blouse with denim jeans that would go perfect with my white Nike shoes.

"We also got you some hot chips because I know you don't want to go back to the lunchroom."

"Where's the twins?" I asked.

"They were gonna fight Aryanna for pulling that stunt and the milk got on their clothes too. But they held them back, now they're all in the office."

Kay-Kay said, "I bet she's gonna claim it was an accident and nobody is gonna talk because they don't want no smoke with Aryanna."

Why is everyone afraid of her?

"Anyways, you don't have to go back to the lunchroom. Just try to hang out here, and we'll meet you after school," Kay-Kay said.

"OK."

They left the restroom as I started to change clothes.

***

I just closed my locker after putting my wet clothes in there. I didn't know where to go since the bell was going to ring in two minutes, so I just hung around my locker. As I was eating my chips, I heard a voice behind me saying, "Hey."

I turned around, and I was stunned.

JaQuan Watts…

"How are you doing?"

I looked around to make sure he was talking to me.

Jaquan chuckled. "Yes, I am talking to you."

I just stood there. I didn't know what to say. I mean, guys came up to me but never one of my crushes.

"You're OK?" he asked.

"Y-y-yeah. I'm fine," I stuttered. Again. *Why? Why did I do that? Now I'm going to be the weird stuttering girl.*

"Are you sure?" JaQuan asked. "Because I heard what happened in the lunchroom, and I was just checking on you."

Oh, no!

Oh, no!

Oh, no!

Now, I'm going to be known as the milk girl.

"So, are you OK?"

Oh God, I was supposed to answer.

Don't stutter.

"Yeah. I'm fine."

Yesss.

"That's good. I'm not sure if you remember my name. But I'm in Mr. Wright's class. I'm JaQuan."

I know. I daydreamed about you every day. By the way, you have a beautiful name.

OK. OK. OK.

You can do this. Just like how you practice at home.

"Hi, I'm Starr."

"OK, Starr. Cute name."

AHHHHHHHHHHHHHHHHH!!

"Thanks."

"I heard you're from California. I need to visit over there. I heard it's beautiful."

"It is. I miss it sometimes."

"Why do you say that?"

"I just miss being able to go to the beach and watch the sunset. I miss the scenery. I miss seeing the skaters riding up and up and down the street. I sometimes miss the people."

"Yeah, I know that can be hard. Not being able to see your old friends or your boyfriend every day."

I chuckled. I knew what he was doing.

I chuckled a bit. "No, I don't have a boyfriend."

"Oh, OK. I apologize. It just seems like you're the type to always have a boyfriend."

I wish I was.

"Nope. No boyfriend."

My face was running hot. I hoped he didn't notice that I was turning red.

JaQuan cleared his throat, "So, um, Starr—"

RIIIIINNNNNNNNGGGGG.

I thanked God because I felt like I was gonna burst because I was actually talking to my crush.

"Well, I guess, we should go to class," I said.

"Oh, what class is it?"

"Biology. Mrs. Hall."

"Oh, I have a class near there. Can I walk you to class?"

I looked at him and was shocked.

I don't know what to do.

How can I respond to that?

I don't know if I can do it. I should say no.

No, Starr, you might not get an opportunity like this again.

Breathe.

I gave a quick breath and said, "Sure."

As we were walking, we talked a little bit more.

"So, how are you liking Birmingham and Alabama so far?" he asked me.

I cleared my throat to say, "Um, it's good." I thought about something else to talk about. "Thought it would be racist at first, but it's cool."

Now, why would I say that? I could've said something else that was interesting.

"Yeah. You do get some racism around here. Especially in places like Mountain Brook and Hoover."

Really?

"Really?"

"Yeah. It's still around, you just need to know where to go."

"OK. I'll be on the lookout."

I felt so sad when we reached our classroom because I wanted to talk to him more.

"OK, thanks for walking with me. See ya'."

"Actually, um, would you like me to walk with you after school? I would like to get to know you," he asked.

OMG! OMG! OMG! OMG!

Should I say yes?

No, I can't do it. I'll stutter and mess it up.

No, no. Breathe.

Wait, he's a basketball player.

"Um, I thought you would have practice."

"I did, but it got canceled. So, is that a yes?"

No. No. Say no. You can't do it. Say no.

"Yeah."

Whyyyyyyyyyyy would you do that?

"Great, I'll meet you in front of the school."

"Great." *Say something since YOU said yes.* "See you then."

"Well, hold up, can I get your number?"

AHHHHHHHH!!! A boy asked for my number. A cute boy at that!

"Um, sure."

He handed his phone to me to lock in my number. I gave his phone back to him, and then he said, "Cool. I'll text you when we get out of school."

Girl, breathe, and be cool.

"OK, I'll be on the lookout for your text," I replied to him.

"Alright, beautiful," he said as he walked away.

He called me beautiful.

As class was going on, I wasn't paying attention. I just wrote my poems, thinking about JaQuan, and how he thought I was beautiful. For the rest of the school day, I was grinning, and for that moment, I didn't care what anybody said.

***

*B*RIINNNGGG!

I usually waited until everyone left before I exited the classroom, but I wanted to meet up with JaQuan before I missed him. After putting my books up in the lockers, I went to the restroom to look to make sure I looked alright. As I was about to walk out, I heard familiar voices saying, "But, did you have to do that girl like that? She did nothing wrong to you."

I realized it was Rayanna, one of Aryanna's minions. That meant she was probably with *her*.

I didn't want her to see me, so I quickly went to one of the stalls and locked it.

"Because she is fat, ugly, and a darkie. All I did was tell her the truth."

From what I heard, they were using the restroom as they were saying awful things about the girls in school. Making fun of girls' hair, body shape, their acne scars on their faces, and their teeth. It made my stomach crawled.

As they used the sink, Katrina said, "Now, wassup with you and the new girl? She just got here, and you already made her life here hell."

"Because she laughed when that punk teacher was trying to embarrass me, so I embarrassed her. Plus, she stuttered. S-sh-she weird," Aryanna told her.

"But other people in there were laughing at you, not just her. Besides, I heard her talk before. She doesn't stutter. Maybe she just fumbled her words."

"I don't care about everyone else or how she sounds. She's new, so she doesn't know who really runs this school. I'm just letting her get the message."

The sink turned off, and Rayanna said, "Don't you think she got it by now?"

"I think she does. I just want to keep messing with her."

"You're so mean," Katrina said.

"Well, call me the black and hood version of Regina George."

I could feel myself shaking as I heard them leaving the restroom. I exited the stall and headed to the mirror. I was just looking at myself, trying not to cry.

Don't cry.

Don't cry.

Breathe.

I got a text notification, and it read:

+12059992121: Hey, I'm out front. Are you alright?

JaQuan.

Me: *I'm coming. Had to use the restroom.*

+12059992121: Alright, beautiful.

I looked at the mirror to make sure I was good before leaving and heading to the front.

Chapter Five

"Hey," I said as I walked up to JaQuan.

"Hey, Starr," he said when he looked up from his phone. "For a moment there, I thought you would ditch me."

Trust me, I thought about that a lot before I got out here.

"No, I wouldn't do that to you," I told him.

"OK, alright, well, after you."

We were walking, and it was silent for a second, and I wanted to start the conversation, but I couldn't.

Girl, push yourself and start talking.

But breathe first.

So, I took a breath and started talking,

"So, did you have a good day?"

"It was good," JaQuan replied. "Glad I don't have practice today."

"Well, aren't you the star player? I thought you'd be living and breathing basketball."

Jaquan chuckled a bit. "Sometimes, I need a break from it. Just relax and have fun."

"Yeah, I understand that; I get like that. When I was a cheerleader with long practi—"

"Wait, you used to cheer?"

Oh. Why did I let that out?

I don't usually talk about it, but, yes, I used to be a cheerleader.

An All-Star cheerleader to be exact. The difference between regular sports team cheerleading and the All-Star cheerleading was that regular sports teams were about cheering on your team, hyping up the crowd, and having cheers and chants. All-Star cheering was none of that. All-

Star cheering focused on competition and skills. It was all about stunts, tumbling, and performances.

"Yeah, I was. But I stopped."

"Why?"

Girl, just because you're a cheerleader, doesn't make you special…

"It's complicated."

"OK, I understand, but you know they're looking for someone to fill in a spot."

"Oh, really?"

I acted interested, but I swore to myself to never return to that sport.

"Yeah, they need a new member since Aryanna quit the team."

I stopped in my tracks.

JaQuan turned to me when I said, "What?"

"OK, I know what you're thinking. Her? As a cheerleader?"

I started back walking with him, and he explained.

"See, she tried out, and she made the squad. But during their summer practices, apparently, she and the captain were having problems. Then, one day they got into it, so she quit."

I bet she did.

"Yeah, so, if you want to."

"Thanks, I'll think about it."

NOT!

We got to know each other more as we continued to walk.

JaQuan is the only child, his parents had been married for twenty years, and he had been playing basketball since he was three. His favorite NBA team were the Atlanta Hawks, but his favorite player was Ja Morant. We had a little back and forth because my favorite team were the Lakers, and Kobe was my favorite player (RIP). His dad was a certified public accountant with his own business, and his mom was an OBGYN.

I never talked to a boy for this long, and I hadn't stuttered once.

Before we knew it, we made it in front of my house.

"Well, this is my home," I said to him.

JaQuan took a look at it and said, "This is a nice home."

"Probably not as big as yours."

"It's OK. Sometimes, I prefer a smaller house anyways."

We stood there for a minute before I asked him, "Are you going to be OK walking home by yourself."

"It'll be alright, once I get a car for my sixteenth birthday."

"Oh, when is it?"

"September 17th."

September 17th. He's a Virgo. Virgos and Aries are good pairs for dating.

"Oh, OK. What's the plan?"

"You'll have to come to find out."

"I can come—I mean, I'll be there." I blushed in embarrassment.

"Cool, so I'll give the details at a later date, and I'll text you when I make it home."

"OK! Thanks for walking me home."

He gave me a hug. "You're welcome, beautiful. Have a good weekend, and I'll see you on Monday."

"Thanks, you too, and see you on Monday."

I walked to the house and went straight to my room. I just grabbed a pillow and screamed from happiness into the pillow because of what happened.

***

I laughed as my momma told me about her day at work as we were sitting in the dining room.

"So, wait a minute. He thought he was going to get your number even after you told him you were married?"

"Yeah!" my momma exclaimed. "Then, he had the nerve to tell me, 'He doesn't have to know. I'll be your sugar daddy.'"

I laughed out loud.

"Like sir, you are old enough to be my daddy, and what are you gonna do with me with them social security checks?"

I couldn't stop laughing because with her being a CNA, she always brought home the tea from the retirement home.

"And get this," my momma continues, "Why does he have a girlfriend at the center?"

"Oop. Not a girlfriend."

"A whole girlfriend, staying down the hall from him."

I kept laughing, and then I heard a vibration on my phone. I immediately grabbed my phone and was disappointed that it was another email. It was after six, and I hadn't heard from JaQuan since he left. I was trying not to let my anxiety get the best of me. I would text to check in on him but if I did, I might double text, and he might think I'm weird.

"Expecting someone to call you?"

"Just either Lauren or Kay-Kay."

"So, how is school coming?"

Besides the fact that a girl is ready to take my head off and what I thought would be my future husband, has basically ghosted me?

"It's good."

"How are you dealing with your anxiety?"

"I'm doing fine with it."

"I heard from Kay-Kay you're making new friends. Do they know?"

"No."

I honestly didn't like talking about my anxiety or telling people about it. Because I didn't want people to feel sorry about me or treat me any differently.

"You're enjoying your new school?"

Besides Aryanna...

"It's OK."

"Well, let's hope that it's better than your old school."

"Yeah. Me too."

After we finished our conversation, I went up to my room, and I felt a vibration on my phone. I look at it and it reads,

Kay-Kay 🖤: *Hey, call me.*

I called her.

"*Giiiirrrrrrlllllllllll,*" that's the first thing she said when she picked up the phone. "What is this I'm hearing that people saw you walking and talking to JaQuan?"

"First off, hello to you, too."

"Hey. Now, is it true, or not?"

I laughed. "Yes, it is."

Kay-Kay screamed over the phone so loud, it started to hurt my ear.

"OK, OK, OK. You're making me deaf early."

"My bad. How did that happen?"

I explained how he came up to me, asked for my number, and walked me home.

"I can't believe you actually pulled him. He doesn't ask anyone out because he's so focused on school and basketball. But I'm happy for you."

"But I don't know if he likes me."

"Why do you say that?"

"After walking me home, he said he would text me when he gets home."

"Maybe he got busy. Hold on, Lauren is calling. Let me merge her in."

I paused for a moment when I heard Lauren saying, "Girl, you're only a week in and you bag one of the most popular boys in the school."

"I didn't bag him," I said.

"If you keep doing what you're doing, you will."

"Well, I don't think that's enough."

"Why do you say that?"

"Because he didn't text her back," Kay-Kay jumped in.

"Girl, if you don't text him back," Lauren said.

"I don't want to text him because I might say something weird. Besides, he said he'll text me, so I'll wait."

Then, Kay-Kay responded, "What if he doesn't?"

"I'll text him in the morning," I answered.

"Babbby, nooo," Lauren spoke up. "You said that he will text you, so you will not text him."

"But what if he forgot?" I asked.

"Then, he should've remembered," Kay- Kay said.

"Oh, my God," I said, "Y'all actin' like my momma right now."

"I'm already your cousin, and I'm already like a sister to you. So, think of me being your overprotective, crazy sister."

"And I'm your classy, bougie, and ratchet-when-needed sister." Lauren said, "Also, Amber is the I-don't-care sister, and Ashley is the nice-but-don't-try-me sister."

"What about me?" I asked.

Kay-Kay replied, "You sweet, good-hearted sister."

"But I don't want to be that."

"Too bad," Lauren said. "That's who you are."

I got a text notification, and it read:*+12059992121: Hey, sorry, I didn't text you. My mom was bugging me about my birthday party, and I forgot to text you. But, how are you doing, beautiful?"*

I squealed.

"What? What's wrong?" Kay-Kay asked.

"He just texted me. What should I say? What should I do? I don't know what to say or what to do? Wha—"

"Whoa, whoa, whoa, calm down, Starr," Lauren said. "Don't overreact. Just text him back.

Oh God, my anxiety is showing. Again.

"Yeah," I said. "You're right—"

Boop!

I looked on the phone and someone was calling me from a number that I didn't know. 205-999-...*OH, IT'S HIM!*

"Oh, my God! He's calling me!"

"Oh, snap!" Lauren yelled.

"Girl, go ahead!" Kay-Kay exclaimed.

"Bye, love y'all!"

"Bye!" they both said before I hung up on them.

I started to sweat, and my stomach started to hurt all of a sudden. I was really debating on declining his call. But if I did, he would probably think I was mad at him or something. But if I did answer, what would I say? Would I stumble again? What if I said something stu—

Girl, you're worrying again. Breathe, and answer the call.

So, I did. "Hello?" I spoke.

"Hello, Starr?"

"Yes?"

"Hey, it's JaQuan."

"Hey."

There was a moment of silence. *Girl, say something.* "So, umm, how are you?"

"I'm good," he replied. "Sorry about not texting you. My mom was bugging me about my birthday party, and I forgot. But I figured after sending the text, it's better for me to call you to explain myself to you. I felt like I owe you that."

"Oh," I said. "You don't have to do that."

"I know, but I want to make it up to you."

All I felt was butterflies in my stomach after he said that. I didn't know what to say after that. I had never been on the phone with a boy before. Now, I had to say something.

Say something, girl.

"Um..." *Um??* "That's um, that's so sweet.... of you."

Great job, you sound awkward.

"You know, I try, I try."

Try to keep the conversation going.

"So, umm, how is the party planning going?"

"It's going good. I'm thinking about having a all-white theme."

"Oh, that would be nice."

"Yeah, I have a couple of nice white suits to consider."

"Oh, wow! Can I see?"

"Nawl, can't do that."

"Why?"

"Because I want it to be a surprise to the guests."

"Oh wow, not even a peek?"

"Nope."

We both laughed.

"OK, I respect that."

"So, when was the last time you had a boyfriend?"

What am I supposed to say? What if he thinks that I'm weird for—no, no, no. Breathe and be honest.

"So, um, I never had a boyfriend."

"For real? You're beautiful. Who wouldn't want to date you?"

Guys who thought I was weird back at home.

"Just… no one has asked me out, yet."

"Well, it's really unfortunate that anyone can deny you. You're really pretty, and you seem like a good person."

I was blushing over the phone.

"Thanks."

"To be honest, I would love to know who Starr really is. If you don't mind."

I felt my heart beating so fast, and I could feel myself starting to sweat. *A boy wants to get to know me. Better yet, JaQuan really wants to get to know me.* I calmed myself down to say, "Sure. What do you want to know?"

"Everything."

Chapter Six

"So, are y'all talking, or just friends?" Kay-Kay asked.

We were in Mr. Wright's class, waiting on class to start.

"Right now, we're talking," I replied.

To be honest, I didn't know what we were. We had been talking the past couple of days, and it was wonderful. We talked about our families, our classes, his basketball stuff, and what to watch. We pretty much talked about everything. Except for my anxiety. I didn't want to tell him just yet.

"Well, I just want you to be careful," Lauren said.

"Why do you say that?"

"Listen, you're a sweetheart and very, very pretty. But think about it, of all the girls in this school, why go to the new girl?"

I really hadn't thought about it like that. *I knew it was too good to be good.*

"Now, Lauren," Kay-Kay jumped in the conversation. "You already know that most of the girls in the school are thots and only want to get with him because he's a potential NBA star. Why would he even go to that?"

"I second that notion," Mark said.

"Now, Mark, what do you know about thots?"

"I know not to trust them."

"Anyways," Lauren said. "I'm just saying. Guys at this school are for everybody and will get with any girls in the school who are vulnerable and don't know the ropes around here. Starr is like the perfect target. Look at D-Rod, for example."

She did have a point. D-Rod had been trying to talk to me, and I was rushing to get out of the conversation or one of my friends would come to save me.

"But JaQuan is not even that type of guy," Kay-Kay said. "He may have talked to like one or two girls, but he hasn't really dated since Kaylyn before she moved last year."

He did tell me about Kaylyn. They dated for almost two years before she moved to Atlanta when her mom got a new job.

"Yeah, my boy doesn't do anything but chill, schoolwork, and play basketball," Mark said.

Lauren looked at Mark and said, "Umm, Mark, this was an A and B conversation. C your way out of black people business."

That's when TJ and Jake came in wearing football jerseys for the first home game tonight.

"Hey, TJ," Mark said. "Since Lauren says to stay out of black people's business, can you please tell her and Starr that JaQuan is a good dude and not out there like that?"

I laughed because I couldn't believe he actually did that.

"Seriously?" Lauren asked as she gave him a death look.

"Hey, you said it, not me."

TJ and Jake laughed, then Myles said, "Yeah, he's cool. Nothing to worry about."

Lauren rolled her eyes.

"So, are you guys ready for tonight?" I asked Jake and Myles.

"Yep," Jake said. "Those boys were talking too much junk these last couple of weeks, so we're gonna see if they can back it up."

"OK, Jake!" Lauren said. "I see you."

"How come he got the special treatment?"

"Because I actually like him."

"Oh, wow!"

We all laughed.

TJ walked up to my desk to hug me and said, "You're good?"

"I'm good. Hope you guys win tonight."

"Yeah, us too. Hope you'll come."

I didn't know if I'd be going to the game until Lauren stepped up to say, "Oh, she'll be there. Especially since I will be dancing on the field during halftime."

I shrugged my shoulders and said to TJ, "I guess I'll be there tonight."

"Alright, bet!" TJ said as he walked to his desk.

I took out my notebook and started writing my poems before class started. Then I heard, "Hey, Starr."

I looked to my right, and it was JaQuan standing beside me.

"Oh, hey," I said to him. *God, he is sooooo fine with his fit.*

JaQuan looked at me confused.

Oh no, what did I do?

"Just 'hey', no hug? So, the football players can get a hug, but not the basketball star?"

"Don't be jealous, Watts," TJ said behind me.

They both laughed, and I chuckled a bit too. I was glad he was playing because I didn't know if he was serious.

JaQuan turned back to me and asked, "So, where's my hug?"

"You didn't ask for it nicely," I flirted.

"Oh, so, I've got to ask now? OK, I see how you do. But, may I have a hug, beautiful?"

I looked at Lauren and Kay-Kay, and we were screaming through our eyes. But I remained cool.

"Sure."

I got up and gave him a hug. His hugs made me forget about the real world for a moment, and his cologne sent me to Heaven.

"Aww, well, ain't that sweet."

That voice suddenly brought me down to Earth.

We let go of each other and saw Aryanna and her crew in front of the class. They were just laughing, making lovey-dovey faces, mocking us.

"JaQuan, I didn't know she's your girlfriend."

JaQuan replied, "Chill out, Ary. She's just a friend."

I'll admit that those words were crushing to me.

"Oh, my bad. Just thought you usually go for the lit girls and not the duds."

Kay-Kay stood up. "OK, what's your problem, Aryanna?"

"No problem. Just pointing out facts."

"OK, Ary. Just drop it," JaQuan said.

"It's OK, JaQuan. I was talking." Aryanna turned to me, and I was sweating, and my stomach was flipping . "Besides, me and Starr are good. Ain't that right, new friend?"

I wanted to throw up because this girl literally said that she wanted to make my life here hell. Now, she was talking about being her friend? I felt my chest starting to hurt. I felt like I couldn't breathe.

"What's wrong, Starr? You OK?" Aryanna said. "Don't get weird on me."

"Y'all don't go near her. She's a weirdo."

"Don't talk to her, bro. She's a weird girl."

"Go away, freak! Nobody wants you!"

I had a mini flashback, and I blacked out for a second, because all of a sudden, I heard, "Come on, Aryanna. Stop doing all that," JaQuan said.

"Yeah, so how about you leave her alone?" Kay-Kay said.

"I didn't even do anything wrong," Aryanna said. "Right, Starr?"

I just wanted to deescalate the situation and be left alone. So, I said, "It's OK, y'all. We're cool."

"See, no harm done, guys."

She is such a witch.

The bell rang, then Mr. Wright came in and said, "Alright, everyone take your seats, we're about to begin. Rory and Theresa, I hope you're all prepared for your presentation."

As everyone was rushing to take their seats, Aryanna bumped me in the shoulder. "Oops, I'm sorry, *friend*," she said as she sat in her seat.

I knew she wasn't sorry.

***

"*All sophomores, report to the gym for the pep rally. All sophomores, report to the gym for the pep rally.*"
I hated pep rallies. They be so packed with people that it made me want to throw up sometimes. I would wait out in the restroom until it was over. Sometimes, female teachers would find me and force me out. I just found another place to hide. Even when I did go, I just sat behind the crowd so I wouldn't be seen. People would look at me as weird, but I just couldn't do it. But, not anymore. This was a new school, and I was going to step out of my comfort zone and have fun. Even so, it was still scary.

I left the theatre, and I met up with Lauren, the twins, Mark, and Ty.

When I reached them, everyone was bursting with laughter.

"Hey, guys," I said, walking towards them. "What you guys laughing about?"

"Oh hey, Starr," Amber said. "We're just asking Mark if he wants to do the class tug-of-war again."

Ty came over to me, laughing, then replied, "Ayo, Starr. It was so funny. Last pep rally, he decided to volunteer in the class tug-of-war, and we were up against the sophomores. We had them at first, but those sophomore boys got strength, and they pulled so hard, they were dragging some of our classmates. But as everyone was letting go, your boy was still hanging on and was dragged across the floor."

Everyone started laughing as I left my mouth open in shock.

"When I tell you that we were so weak for at least five minutes. Even some of the teachers were weak."

Mark then responded, "That's why I'm not volunteering for nothing. Don't ask me, don't tell me to do anything, because I'm not doing it."

"But, why did you hang on?" I asked. "Why didn't you let go?"

"I don't know what my thought process was back then. I was trying to help, but nobody came to check in to see if I was ok."

Ty looked at Mark and said, "Bruh, you were laughing along with us. So, what are you talking about?"

"Y'all still could've checked on me."

"Man, whatever, let's go."

We started walking when I heard a voice behind me saying, "Hey, Starr, hold up!"

I turned to see JaQuan running to me.

"Hey," I said with slight excitement in my voice.

I looked at my friends and they gave me an "ooh" look, and Lauren said, "We'll see you inside, Starr."

I nodded as they left me with Jaquan. He turned to me.

"Wassup, JaQuan?"

"Nothing much. Hoping to be sitting next to you at the pep rally."

AHHHHHHHHHH...OK. Be cool.

"What about your friends? What are they gonna say when they see that you are with a girl, and not with them?"

JaQuan smacked his lips. "Man, they ain't gonna worry about me. If anything, they'll be happy that I'm actually talking to a girl. Say that I work too much and live my life, but my life is school and basketball."

I chuckled a bit.

"At least you're dedicated."

"Yeah, I am. Let's go find our seats before it gets too full."

***

"Alright, Wildcats, it's tradition that we do this," Mr. Wright, our hype man for the pep rally, said into the mic. "It's time for the class tug-of-war! I need ten freshmen boys and ten sophomore boys."

TJ stood up and pointed at Mark and said, "Come on, Mark!"

Mark stood there and shook his head, saying no. I just started laughing at his reaction.

The pep rally had been fun so far. I got to see Kay-Kay dance with the band, and me and Lauren cheered until our voices became hoarse. We got lit to the DJ, we chanted along with the cheerleaders, and we did a TikTok dance battle that the sophomores won. Of course. I was really enjoying myself besides the few occasions where Aryanna and her friends laughed loudly behind us. Probably talking about me sitting next to JaQuan, but whenever he turned to smile at me, I didn't care about what anyone had to say.

After many attempts, Mark refused to do the tug-of-war. So, the sophomore boys went up and surprisingly won against the freshmen. Then, they went on to beat the juniors. Our girls went up to go against the freshmen girls, but we didn't stand a chance.

Mr. Wright got on the mic again. "Alright, Wildcats. It's time to see which class is the loudest and the littest. It's time for the Class Spirit Stick competition!"

One of the staff brought out a long blue stick that had strings and had the words "WILDCATS" in sparkly colors.

Ty stood up and yelled to our class, "Ay, man, we got to be loud! We got to show them that we're the littest class, alright?"

They all exclaimed, "Yes, sir!"

"We got you."

"Period!"

Then Ty yelled out, "Ay, as soon they're done, everyone stand up and follow my say!"

After the freshmen had their turn, Ty threw his hands up, signaling everyone to get up, and Ty chanted, "Sophomores! Sophomores! Sophomores!"

Soon enough, the whole class caught on. Then, Mr. Wright waved the spirit sticks towards us and yelled, "Sophomores, where you at?"

We made some crazy noise in that gym. Including me. Even the tenth graders who were in the band made extra noise with their instruments.

"Tenth grade, tenth grade, tenth grade!" We all chanted.

"Uh-oh, upperclassmen, you got some competition over here," Mr. Wright said as he moved on to the juniors.

Unfortunately, the seniors won the spirit stick, as we expected.

Mr. Wright asked everyone to come out and support the football team, and the band closed everything off by playing the school's alma mater.

As everyone was starting to leave, I saw Ty looking sad. I told JaQuan to hold on a minute as I went to Ty and said to him, "It's OK. At least we had fun."

I know I did. I would've never known that pep rallies would be that fun. I was so ready for the next one.

Ty looked at me and smiled, "We did."

"You OK?"

"I'm good, thanks though."

He gave me a hug, and as we let go, we heard, "Aww, look at that. Starr has another boyfriend. Wonder how JaQuan would feel."

Aryanna.

"Man, shut up, Aryanna, and mind your business." Ty clapped back as her and her friends walked by, laughing.

I looked down at the ground in embarrassment.

"Hey." I looked up at Ty. "I got you. But, you really need to tell someone about her."

"I will." Even though I probably wouldn't.

"You better."

I gave him a little smile and walked to meet up with JaQuan in the hallway.

"You're ready?" he asked.

"Yep."

Chapter Seven

"Remember to call me when the game is about to be over," my mom asked of me.

"Yes ma'am."

"You got your emergency money, right?"

"Yes ma'am."

"Be sure to give me Lauren's number so if I can't reach you or Kay-Kay, I can contact her."

"Yes ma'am."

"Also, your Auntie Gina is down the street from the school, so if there's a shooting, don't stick around. Call me and go straight to her house."

"Yes ma'am."

This was my first time going to a football game with my friends. Well, this was my first time hanging out with anyone outside my family. So, my mom was more nervous than me because she knew that anything could trigger me into a panic attack.

"Also, your Auntie Gina is down the street from the school, so if there's a shooting, don't stick around. Call me and go straight to her house."

"Yes ma'am."

I walked in the living room where my dad was watching TV while Skylar was playing with Sekani on the couch.

"You look pretty, Starr," Skylar said.

"Awww, thank you, Skylar." I was wearing a black Avondale shirt, some khaki cargo shorts, and a pair of black and white Converse high tops. I looked simple.

"Starr, I'm proud of you," Daddy spoke.

"Proud of me for what?"

"For stepping out of your comfort zone and how far you have been progressing since we moved here. You made some friends, you're going out, and having fun."

I walked to him and hugged him. "Thanks, Daddy."

As I waited for Lauren and the twins, I sat on the couch thinking about what he said, and it brought back memories. Memories from kindergarten.

"How come you don't talk?" Erica Greene said. She was my first torturer. She would make fun of me because I didn't talk to anyone. I was too afraid to talk. I didn't know why. I just didn't talk. I was too afraid to talk in class. My teacher thought once I got over my jitters, I would open up, but that never happened.

I would sit by myself at lunch because I was too afraid to say anything to the kids. My teacher encouraged me to sit with the kids, but every time I got tired, they would move away. That's because Erica would convince the kids that I was weird and not to sit next to me.

"Don't sit next to her. She doesn't talk, and she will stare at you. She's a weirdo." She would say.

BEEEP! BEEEP! I snapped out of my mind to look out the window, and it was my crew. I kissed everyone and said my goodbyes. I walked to the car and sat in the backseat with Ashley, while Amber was driving and Lauren was in the passenger seat.

"Hey, Starr," Lauren spoke up.

"Hey, y'all! Amber, since when did you drive?"

"Man, me and Ashley have been driving," she answered as she pulled off. "We couldn't drive our car until we turned sixteen which was like a week before school started."

"Why are you just now driving?"

"Because our momma wanted us to wait a little while for whatever reason," Ashley replied. "I think she wasn't ready to see us driving."

"Nawl, she was ready for us to drive. I don't think she trusts us to drive. She is paranoid for no reason," Amber said to her sister.

I just laughed at them complaining about their mother the whole ride.

***

"This game is about to jump," Amber said as we sat on the bleachers.

"Yeah. Everyone is out here," Lauren jumped in, carrying the food.

"I'm ready to see Kay-Kay dancing," I spoke up.

"Yeah, she's gonna kill it on the field," Lauren said. "We're gonna embarrass her tonight."

"No, I think my Auntie Gina and my Uncle Jim got it."

"Yeah, I know. I remember one time during a talent show when Kay-Kay was performing a Beyoncé song, and Ms. Gina…"

The conversation faded in my ear when I saw Aryanna and her minions. As they walked by, Aryanna gave me a look and started laughing. I knew that she was laughing at me. I could feel my heart pounding out my chest and I could feel my hand just trembling.

Not now…

Not right now. I was doing good. Remember what you were taught, Starr.

Close your eyes.

Deep breath.

Refocus your attention on what's going on now.

Hanging out with my new friends.

You're at a football game.

You're here to watch Kay-Kay perform.

Breathe.

I opened my eyes when I heard Lauren say, "Uh-oh, look who is coming our way."

61

I turned, and it was JaQuan and some of his teammates walking up the bleachers towards us.

"Good evening, ladies," JaQuan greeted us.

We all replied, saying, "Good evening, JaQuan."

"Mind if we sit and hang with you ladies tonight?"

"Why, I don't know, JaQuan." Ashley answered. "Did you want to hang out with us, or do you want to hang out with my girl, Starr?"

He chuckled and started blushing a bit, which made me smile and blush too.

Ashley laughed too. "See. I knew it."

I looked at him and said, "You can sit with me."

"OOOUUU!" all of our friends exclaimed, embarrassing both of us.

One of his teammates came up and patted him on the shoulder. "Ay, Watts, we spotted our own little boos, so we'll catch up to you after the game."

They dapped it up, left, and he sat next to me.

Why would he sit next to me? He is gonna make me freak out.

To calm me down, I paid attention to the cheerleaders as they were warming up. I was watching one girl toe touch, and I muttered, "She needs to point her touch."

"What you said?" JaQuan asked.

"What? Oh no, I'm talking to myself about cheerleader stuff."

Great, now he thinks I'm weird because I talk to myself.

"Do you miss it?"

"Miss what?"

"Cheering."

I missed it so much. Cheering was my escape. I know it's weird for me to have social anxiety and be an all-star cheerleader, but my mom signed me up for me to make some friends, and I somewhat made two friends. But after the incident, I fell out of love with cheering and quit at twelve.

"Yeah, I do."

JaQuan stood up and reached his hand out towards me. I looked at it for a moment before I grabbed it. He pulled me up, and we walked down the bleachers. I turned to my friends for some help, and they gave me some thumbs up. *Some friends I have.*

We were walking toward a fit lady, who wore a green and gold tracksuit on the field, talking to a few cheerleaders.

She is a coach.

A cheer coach.

I shook my head and tried to pull back, but he pulled me back.

"What's going on, Ms. Kennedy?" JaQuan greeted.

"Hey there, JaQuan." They gave each other a quick hug. "How's basketball coming?"

"It's going alright. Can't wait to see what cheers y'all bring this year."

"You know we finna bring some heat to the bleachers."

"Well, I brought someone who might help you."

"Oh, really?" She turned to look at me. "Is it this pretty girl next to you?"

I smiled.

"Yes, it is." JaQuan pulled me closer to the fence. "Ms. Kennedy, this is Starr. Starr, this is Ms. Kennedy."

She examined me, and I got nervous.

"So, you say she can help me?"

"Yeah, she's just transferred here from LA, and she used to be a-a- what you call it again, Starr?"

"All-Star cheerleader," I reminded him.

"Really?" Ms. Kennedy said with her eyes widened.

I shook my head saying yes.

"What level are you?"

"Oh, uh, four."

"What is your position?"

"I-I can do all positions, but I am mostly a flyer and a back spot."

"Can you tumble?"

This feels like an interview.

I shook my head.

"Hey, Kourtney and Harmony. Come here for a sec."

Two beautiful girls walked up to the fence.

"Starr, this is Kourtney and Harmony, our captain and co-captain. Ladies, this is Starr. She transferred here from LA and was an All-Star cheerleader."

"Hi, I'm Harmony." Harmony was a slim, brown-skinned tall girl. She could be a model.

"Hey, I'm Mariah." Mariah was a light skin tone and kinda short.

Ms. Kennedy turned to them. "Starr seems to be interested in being on our squad, and I think she could be a great addition. Do you girls have a problem with it?"

I looked at Ms. Kennedy in shock.

"I'm fine with it," Mariah said.

Harmony shrugged her shoulders and replied, "I don't have a problem with it."

Can I do this?

No, you can't. You just got here.

"Uh-I-well, I can wait until next year to try out, since the season has already started. Besides, I never cheered at games before."

"You can learn," Ms. Kennedy assured me. "I don't know about football, but we can definitely use you for basketball season. Why don't you come to our practice on Monday?"

I am stunned.

"Um, well, I don't know. I'm still new here, and I'm just trying to get used to my new routine. Plus, I haven't tumbled or stunted in three years and—"

"Come on, Starr," JaQuan pleaded. "You just said you missed it. Plus, you can cheer for me at my games."

The thought of me cheering for him was enough to make my face turn red. I turned to Ms. Kennedy and shook my head in agreement.

"Perfect! Our practice starts promptly at 3:30 on the field. Be sure to be there on time."

"Yes, ma'am."

I waved at the other girls and walked up to my friends who were joined by Mark and Blu.

"So, what happened?" the twins said in unison.

I loved it when they did that. It was funny and cute.

"JaQuan set me up, y'all," I chuckled.

"I'm setting her up to be great. At least she gets to practice with the cheerleading squad."

The girls gasped, squealed, and got up to hug me.

I didn't know how to feel about the group hug. It was like I wanted to say 'please get off of me', but I loved it.

"I'm so happy for you!" Lauren exclaimed. "Kay-Kay is a dance girl, and you're gonna be a cheerleader. Now, what am I gonna do?"

"You got us," the twins said.

"You got me, too," Blu stated as he jumped in the conversation.

"Um, no." Lauren responds back.

"Come on, Lauren, give my man a chance," JaQuan said.

"I will be in another universe."

"That's cold, Lauren," Blu laughed. "It's OK though. I'm gonna manifest you being my girl."

"Ooooouuuuuuu," we all gushed.

Lauren was about to say something when we heard drums. It was the band marching in. We all hurried to the gate to catch Kay-Kay in action. Here she comes, wearing a golden bodysuit majorette uniform, coming down the track.

We all screamed her name and recorded her as she was marching. I saw my Auntie Gina and Uncle Jim walking along with band parents, and I waved at them. They smiled and waved back at me as Kay-Kay got to her spot on the bleachers. Seeing my cousin, my best friend dancing, was one of the best moments for me.

"Go, Kay-Kay!" Auntie Gia said as we cheered my cousin on during her halftime routine.

We all were standing on our feet throughout the entire halftime routine. I loved every moment of it. I was very proud of her.

Once it was over, we cheered for her and the band, and we made our way back to our seats.

"Now, it's back to watching this sorry game," Blu complained.

The score was 21-7. We were losing.

"Wow, what a way to show school spirit, Blu," Lauren sarcastically said.

"I'm just speaking the truth, sweetheart."

"You can have faith. You know your friends are on the team too, right?"

They kept arguing like a couple, and I let JaQuan know that I had to go to the restroom.

***

As I was washing my hands, the door opened, and Aryanna, Katrina, and Rayanna came in. I froze, and my hands just started trembling.

"W-w-wassup, S-s-s-stuttering Starr?" Aryanna laughed.

I gathered enough energy to speak up.

"Look…I don't want any trouble."

"Oh, well, I do. A little birdie told me that you're gonna take what used to be my spot."

I looked down at the ground. "I'm not trying to take anyth—"

"Yes, you are!" she snapped as she walked closer to me. "Trying to be like me. You think you can come here and take my spot and try to take my place at the school? Nawl, it ain't finna go down like that. Not with me around."

I could feel myself about to cry, but I couldn't do it in front of them.

"I've also seen you and JaQuan, laughing and smiling with each other. So, what's the deal with y'all?"

Breathe, Starr, don't break down.

"We're just friends," I responded lowly.

"What's that? I can't hear you." She was getting closer to my face.

"We're just frie—"

"I'm sorry, I still can't hear you with your mousy—"

"I said we're just friends!"

I felt a hard punch in my stomach, causing me to crunch down and fall to the floor.

"Who do you think you're talking to?"

I didn't say anything because I was coughing.

Don't do it. Don't do it. Remember the last time you fought. Don't do it.

Aryanna stooped over me and said to me, "I'm gonna say this one time and one time only: stay in your place, and stay away from JaQuan. He's too good for you. What will he think when he sees his 'friend' on the floor crying? Why would he want someone like you?"

Rayanna stepped up and said, "Come on, Ary, we got to go."

"Not until she gets the message."

"Ary, that's enough. Let's go before someone comes in here."

"You better not say nothing." She got up and started to walk out saying, "Weak little girl."

"Why would you do…."

The door slammed.

I slowly got up to the sink and looked in the mirror.

Why does this happen to me?

All I want is to start over and to find myself.

But this cycle is just following me wherever I go.

I quickly grabbed some napkins. I ran the water to splash my face and dried it.

I can't stay at this game.

I got to go home.
I need to get out of here.

I quickly walked out, hoping I wouldn't run into her again. I felt a bump, and I started to panic and hyperventilate thinking it was her, but it turned out to be Ty.

"Whoa, whoa, Starr it's OK. It's me," Ty said to calm me. "You OK?"

"I'm fine," I quickly replied, and I just walked off and made it to the bleachers.

The team just made a touchdown making the score 21-14, and the band just finished playing. I looked up to see all my friends, even JaQuan was having fun and having a good time. Even Blu and Lauren were laughing together.

God, I hate to ruin their fun, but I can't stay here.
What if they think I'm weird because I asked for them to leave when the night is starting to be good?

I looked to find my auntie and uncle, and I saw them by the gate. I walked to them and said, "Hey, Auntie and Unc, I'm not feeling too well. I need to go home."

"Are you sure, sweetheart?" my auntie asked. "Do you need to see one of the band parents who is a nurse? I can call her ov—"

"No. I just need to go home."

Auntie Gina and Uncle Jim looked at each other to find a solution.

"Well, Starr, we don't want to leave Kay-Kay, we can call your mom and she can come…"

"It's OK," Uncle Jim spoke up. "I can take you home."

I felt so much relief.

"You're sure, Jim?"

"Yeah, I was planning on leaving the stadium to go the car and smoke anyway. I'll be back when it's time for her to leave."

As much as I disliked the smell of cigarettes, I had no choice.

"Thank you, Uncle Jim. I'll be telling my friends that I will be leaving."

He nodded, and I headed towards my friends.

"Hey, guys, I'm not feeling good. So, I'll be going home."

"Nooooooooo," Lauren cooed.

"Awww, man, and the game was starting to get good," Blu said.

"I hope you feel better," Mark said.

I felt someone grab my arm. I turned to see it was JaQuan.

"Is everything OK?" he asked me.

My heart was breaking because he was so sweet and so caring, but with Aryanna around, I couldn't be with him.

"It's...just some girl issues."

"Oh, OK. Do you want me to take you home? I don't have a problem wit—"

"No," I unintentionally cut him off. "No. It's OK. My uncle is taking me home."

I turned back to my friends. "Bye, y'all."

They were all saying bye to me when I started to walk away. I walked passed JaQuan when he yelled, "I'll text you later, Starr."

I didn't respond back to him. I kept walking to my uncle, and we went to the car. As he was driving, I looked OUT the window, thinking how my new life had been a dream come true to a real life repeat of a nightmare. We made it to my house, and I told my uncle goodbye and went inside the house. I entered my home to see my family playing a Sonic game on our PlayStation. They all saw me walking in and yelled, "Hey!"

Skylar and Sekani ran up to hug me. They let go to go back to their game. Momma came up and said, "You're home early. Did something happen?"

I was hit in the stomach and was threatened not to talk to my crush.

"No, nothing happened. I was going through some girl stuff and wasn't feeling well."

"Well, what's wrong? Is it a cramp?" Momma came up to me to ask. "Did your cycle come on?"

"No, Momma. Just... I wasn't feeling too well, but I'm starting to feel better."

"So, how was the game? How did Kay-Kay do on the stand? I know she killed it."

"It was good," I lied. "The team was losing at first, but they was making a comeback before I left. Kay-Kay did great! I recorded some of her dancing."

"I'll watch them later. I'm too busy whooping your daddy in Sonic."

"You're not whooping anything because I'm gonna make a comeback on you," Daddy responded to her comment.

"OK, I'm going to bed," I told them.

"You don't want to stay and watch us play?" Skylar said with sad eyes.

God, please don't make me cry.

"Of course, I do, Skylar. But I'm just tired and need to lay down."

Skylar pouted.

God give me strength.

"It's OK, Skylar," Daddy comforted her. "You can still see me making a comeback on your momma."

"Oh, really?" Momma said. "We'll see about that."

I listened to my family having fun as I walked to my room, and it hurt me.

I loved spending time with them, especially when we turned on the PlayStation. I just didn't want them to suspect that something was wrong with me.

I changed clothes and went to bed. My phone was blowing up with texts from the group chat from my friends that the football team was making a comeback and eventually won. Kay-Kay called me twice, but I didn't pick up. JaQuan even text to see if I was OK. I didn't respond. I put my phone down and started crying.

Why is this happening to me again?

Chapter Eight

Los Angeles, 2021

"*S*tarr, *he's looking at you again,*" Destiny whispered to me at the lunch table.

Destiny Harris had been my first and only friend back in California. She was also on my LA All-Star Squad. She had been my back spot in our stunt group. We'd met when we were nine years old, and at first, I wouldn't talk to her much. But she was persistent, and we'd been friends ever since. We did almost everything together. We went to the movies together, went to amusement parks together, had sleepovers, and we even took trips together.

All that changed when we went to the same high school. She had gained more friends and started dating boys. I was kind of left in the dark because she was the only one who knew my social anxiety, and it was hard for me to talk to people. I was pretty much on my own when she almost never invited me to hang with her new friends or go to parties. We still hung out and talked at school, but not as much as we used to.

"*You know I can't do it, Destiny,*" I responded. "*He's probably not interested in me.*"

The boy we were referring to was Antwon Knight. He was a cute guy that was in our grade. We noticed that he was looking at me specifically at lunch.

"*Girl, what are you talking about? You're cute, you're popping. You can pull anyone without even trying.*"

"*But, I don't know if I can go up to anyone, let alone someone like Antwon. They already think that I'm a weird girl with how I stutter when I talk and don't hang out with anyone besides you."*

The "weird girl" tag followed me from kindergarten to now, thanks to Erica Greene. She was the most popular girl in our grade and would do anything to make my life miserable. She would spread lies about me going to different mens' houses because I preferred older men than boys my age. She told people that I didn't have any female friends because I was too fast for them. She even said that I practiced black magic, and I was a witch. It all happened throughout the years, and it was getting worse.

"I spoke to Antwon before, and he doesn't think that. He actually thinks you're cute."

"Seriously?"

"Yeah, he even asked if you were single."

"Oh, my God, Destiny. Are you serious?"

"As a heart attack." She looked at him and signaled him to come over.

I saw him walking over, and I instantly panicked. Destiny grabbed my hands and told me, *"Starr, calm down."*

I calmed down. She let go of my hands.

"Just breathe and be you." She walked away.

Breathe.

"Hey, Starr," Antwon said as he walked up to the table.

"H-Hi." OMG why did I stutter?

"How are you?"

Say something, Starr.

"I'm good."

"That's good. Do you mind if I sit right here?"

Before I can say yes, here comes the trouble.

"Don't even waste your breath, Antwon," Erica Greene commented. *"You're only going to find out how weird she is. Plus, she is probably too busy with her grown boyfriend. So, she probably is not interested in young guys."*

At that moment, and I don't know where I got that energy from, but I finally snapped. I slammed my hand on the top and got up and yelled, *"What's your problem with me!"*

The whole lunchroom became silent, and I was shocked. I never thought I could get that loud. Erica was shocked, but she just started laughing.

"Ooooouuu, look at that. I finally know what you sound like when you're not talking low."

At that point, I didn't care if my crush was near me or who was watching. I got up and went to her face because I was tired of her.

"What's your issue with me? Why do you keep messing with me? I didn't do anything to you."

"Because I want to. You don't talk to anyone, you s-s-s-stutter when you talk, you don't talk to boys, you don't have any friends, and you always get pulled from class to go to one of those retarded classes."

Those "retarded" classes that she was referring to, was my speech therapy. I had an IEP plan because of my social anxiety. I had to go to a school-appointed speech therapist to help with my stuttering, I had to go to the front office to take a break in a quiet space, and I got extra time on assignments and tests just so I wouldn't get overwhelmed, and I had a transition plan on how I moved from class to class.

Not only was she saying I was slow, but she was calling people with disabilities the R word. I could feel my hands trembling, and my heart was racing. I legit wanted to hurt this girl. But, I wasn't trying to get suspended for her or anybody.

Stand your ground, Starr. Everyone is watching. Prove them wrong.

"That's none of your business on what I do during or after school. I go straight home and do my homework. If you didn't party every weekend, you might have a good chance on passing your classes."

Everyone started ooh-ing and cracking up. She switched from smiling to embarrassed to angry real quick.

"So, you think you're better than me, weirdo?"

Everyone was starting to gather around. I could feel my heart beating fast, and I was seeing red. Then, I could hear my momma's voice saying, *"If you can get out of an altercation, walk away."*

"For the last time, stop calling me that."

"Or what?" She pushed me.

It took me a second to realize what happened. I had seen fights that started off like this at school and in my neighborhood. But I never thought that I would be in a situation like this. I don't know if I wanted to run or fight. But I heard my momma saying, *"However, if they hit you, you better hit them back."*

I took a breath and told her straight up, *"Don't push me again. I'm not trying to fight."*

"But I do." She pushed me again. This time I lost it. The next thing I remembered was being in the principal's office. My principal recapped what I did. Apparently, after she pushed me, I punched her dead in her face, and she fell back. But, I kept hitting and kicking her while she was on the ground, and she ended up being temporarily unconscious and having a concussion. I can't lie; I was happy and didn't regret that I fought her.

My parents were called and informed them that I was suspended for a week, which made them furious.

They rushed to the school to confront the principal about Erica's bullying. Yes, they knew about Erica. All the way from elementary school, they had reported this girl for years for bothering me and making up stories about me. Nobody did anything about it. The principal swore up and down that she never received any reports on her. Figures. My momma argued with the principal that what I did was self-defense. But because after she hit the ground and I kept hitting her, it was no longer self-defense, so I was suspended for a week for giving her what she deserved. The fight went viral on social media and was all over the school. You would think that I was going to be respected by my peers and show them that I wasn't a "weirdo" right? Wrong.

Because of how this girl was loved, I became public enemy #1 at that school. Antwon would avoid me because he didn't want to be associated with me. The bullying got ten times worse. They would put sticky notes on my lockers, calling me all types of names, they would taunt me in the hallway, put gum in my hair, try to corner me in the bathroom trying to fight, and just made my life there hell on earth. And you might ask, where was Destiny? She was nowhere to be found. She would rather hang out with her new friends and her new boyfriend than me. The cyberbullying was horrible. I didn't like to talk about it because it would make me have suicidal thoughts.

My parents did everything they could to make it stop. Multiple parent meetings, going to school board meetings, even tried going to the state board. There were only three suspensions, but nothing much came out of it. Eventually, my dad put in a request to transfer from LA to Birmingham, AL where his family is. We started the moving process before the school year was over. On the day we were moving, Destiny came by.

"So, you're really leaving?" Destiny asked as I brought my stuff outside.

"Yep," I said it coldly.

"And you weren't going to tell me bye?"

"I didn't think you'd care."

"Of course, I care," Destiny chuckled. *"I'm still your friend."*

I paused. Is she serious right now?

"If you're my friend, where were you when everyone was against me?"

She stood there and didn't respond to that question.

"If I was your friend, where were you when I almost got jumped in the bathroom, or when they came at me online? I had to delete all my social media. I quit the All-Star team

because I didn't want people to know where I be goin' So, tell me, how are you still my friend?"

I resumed moving my stuff to the truck.

Destiny finally responded. *"You should've said something to me. I would've done something."*

I stopped again. *"You knew what was happening because half of the main people that were tormenting me were* your *friends. So don't tell me that, Destiny."*

"What was I supposed to do, Starr? You fought the girl, and she ended up with a concussion."

"Because she was bullying me ever since kindergarten. I didn't want to fight her, but when she pushed me again, I just snapped."

Destiny was stunned. *"Starr, I didn't know."*

"Of course, you didn't. You were too busy with everyone else but me. But, it's OK. I'm used to being alone."

"You still could've told me."

"I didn't because cheering and hanging out with you was my only escape from school and from her. I wanted to tell you about her, but you weren't paying any attention to me when we started at Crenshaw. But I don't blame you. I'm just a retarded weirdo that doesn't talk at all, has a stuttering problem, and has violent tendencies. So, why hang out with me, huh?"

I was on the verge of tears because at that moment, I felt like I had no one.

"Starr, I don't know what to say. I'm sorry."

"Yeah, me too."

I continued to load my stuff to the moving truck, and when I looked behind me, she was gone. That was the last time I saw or spoke to her. To be honest, it was good. Because there was no going back on our friendship. I was ready for a new start in a new town and to leave my past behind me. But little did I know, that dark shadow would follow me.

Chapter Nine

"Come on, Starr! You're gonna be late!" my momma yelled from the bottom of the steps. After I finished putting my hair up in a ponytail, I looked at myself in the mirror. I was feeling so down this past weekend. I hadn't responded back to anyone, not even Kay-Kay. But, I saw everyone's Snapchat and Instagram, and they were all having fun at the game. I hate that I missed it. I came downstairs just to grab an apple. I didn't have much of an appetite.

"You got everything?" my mom asked as she put Sekani's shoes on in the living room.

"Yes ma'am."

"You're not forgetting anything?"

"No, I don't think so."

"What about practice clothes and some water?"

I stared at her. *How did she know?*

"I know you may be wondering how I knew? Well, Kay-Kay told Auntie Gia, and your Auntie Gia asked me if it was true."

I didn't say anything but took another bite.

Momma asked, "Baby, why didn't you say anything?"

I shrugged my shoulders before I answered. "I don't know if I can do it. Besides, maybe it's best for me not to do it this year since I'm still new."

Momma picked Sekani up and came up to me.

"Baby, the main reason that your daddy and I named you Starr is because you were born to shine."

I chuckled a bit.

"No lie, when the doctors put you in my arms, I felt nothing but brightness from the inside. Also, you came out bright. People would mistake you as a white baby."

We both started laughing.

"But, in all seriousness, with everything that happened to you back in LA, when you were competing, I saw the brightness come out of you. You love cheerleading, and it brings you happiness. So don't let the past or anyone make you steer away from it."

Unless it's Aryanna.

"But it's entirely up to you. But I got your new practice clothes in that red bag in the corner."

With a minute of thinking, I grabbed the bag and walked out the door.

***

"Starr," Kay-Kay called my name as she and Lauren approached me in the hallway when I just opened my locker. "We have been calling and texting you all weekend. You missed a lot. What's going on with you?"

"I wasn't feeling well," I lied. "It was probably a stomach bug. But I'm fine now. So, what did I miss?"

"Lauren and Blu went on a date on Saturday."

My mouth dropped as I turned to Lauren.

"It was not a date," Lauren clarified. "We just went out to have a burger."

"Sounds like a date to me," I commented.

"Man, shut up," Lauren laughed.

Kay-Kay asked, "So, what was it then?"

"Just friends, where one has a crush on the other, hanging out at a burger joint on a Saturday."

"A date," me and Kay-Kay said together.

"Man, whatever," Lauren said.

BRIIIIIINNNNNGGGGGGG.

"See you at lunch." Kay-Kay turned to me and nodded her head. They walked away.

I grabbed some books out of my locker and closed it. As I started walking, I felt a hard push behind me. I fell face down and heard some laughing behind me. I turned around to see who it was.

"M-M-My bad, Starr." It was Aryanna. Behind her was Rayanna, Katrina, and D-Rod.

"Ay man, leave her alone." D-Rod came to my defense.

They walked passed me, and I got up to pick up my books and notebook. But someone came and helped me. It was Ty. I stood up and asked, "Did you see?"

"Yeah, I saw," he answered as he gave me the rest of my stuff. "Starr, you should really tell someone—"

"No," I cut him off. "I can't get anyone in trouble over me. Please don't say anything."

"Starr—"

"Please," I begged.

Ty let out a huge sigh and said, "OK, but I'll still say you should tell somebody."

"I'll figure something out."

What is that something? I don't know.

***

I was on my way to lunch when I heard voices in the hallway.

"But for real, what's your beef with her?" That sounded like D-Rod.

"Ain't no beef. Just want to let her know who really runs this school." That was Aryanna. I stopped in my tracks, and l hid by the lockers to listen in.

"But, you didn't have to push her."

"Why do you care?"

"I'm just saying, I think she gets the point. So, just chill out."

"You're only saying that because you're feeling her. But, yet, you didn't help her up."

It was silent. I hated saying this, but she had a point right there.

"Trust me when I say, she's not what you want. Did you see how she just sat there after I pushed her? She's a weak, scared, little girl. Why would you want something like that?"

"Maybe because you're scary? You put fear in a lot of people's hearts for no reason. You're starting to be like your momma—"

I heard a locker door slam, which startled me.

"I ain't nothin' like my momma. You keep this up, and everyone will know your situation. Do you want this pick up or not?"

"Yeah, whatever."

"Alright, be sure to bring my percentage on Friday. Also, I got a drop off for you after school."

Drop off? Are they talking about drugs?

"Plus, there's a party where I need you to sell molly and some trees at."

Yep, they're talking about drugs.

I knew a lot about drugs from when Destiny was talking about it when she went to these parties.

"I got you."

"Bet."

I heard footsteps approaching so I walked in a different direction. As I turned a corner, I bumped into someone. It was JaQuan.

"Hey, Starr," he said with a smile.

"Hey…umm, JaQuan," I replied.

"How are you?"

"I'm good."

"That's good. I haven't heard from you, and I want to make sure that you are OK."

At that moment, Aryanna walked past us and said, "Aww. Y'all are cute."

We didn't say anything to her, but I knew what might happen.

"I'm fine, JaQuan," I responded to his concern. "But I gotta go. I'm late for lunch."

"OK, I can walk with you."

"No. That's OK. I can walk alone."

I started walking away in tears. But these questions were still in the back of my head.

Why is she selling drugs?

What situation is D-Rod in?

What is her mother like at home?

Chapter Ten

"OK, ladies," Ms. Kennedy said as we huddled around her as practice was about to end. "We're playing against West End on Friday, and you know their cheerleaders are not to be played with. So, we're only going to put the best on the field, so be prepared for the mock game day practice tomorrow. Also, let's give a huge shout-out to our newcomer, Starr."

Everyone started clapping for me, and I smiled a bit.

"These last few practices have been rough for her to transition from one style of cheerleading to another. But she improved drastically, and she's doing a great job on learning our material in a short time span."

They clapped for me again. It was not easy. With me working out again, learning how to stunt again, learning the dances and actually learning cheers, I was struggling. But thanks to the squad's captains, Kourtney and Harmony, they stayed after practice with me to make sure I got all my words and motions right. I also worked on them at home. Skylar wanted to be a cheerleader, too. I would be teaching her some of our material But, it was a great way for us to bond again.

After practice ended, I was on my way home when I heard someone calling me.

"Ms. Brown!"

I turned, and it was my theater teacher, Ms. Bailey, running up to me.

"Hey, Ms. Bailey."

"Hey, Ms. Brown," she greeted while catching her breath.

"I've been meaning to talk to you after class. But you were in such a hurry, I couldn't catch up with you."

"Yeah, I had cheer practice."

"OK. OK. That's great, but remember our assignment on Spoken Words."

I shook my head.

"So, I read your poem about growing up in LA, and you are actually talented."

"Yeah, been writing since I was young."

"I do, too. Well, anyways, I want to see if you heard about the Black Teen Magazine's Poetry to a Song contest?"

Black Teen Magazine was dedicated to black teens and focused on pop culture, celebrity news, and teen lifestyle. Every year, they would team up with a record company and host a contest to where a teen could turn their poem into a song for a secret celebrity.

"Yeah, I heard of it."

"Well, I think that you should definitely submit something."

I was stunned. I had to think about my answer because the thought of me winning that contest and becoming a songwriter. Not in my own dreams.

"Umm, I don't know about that."

"I mean the deadline isn't until a few weeks from now, but it's something to think about. We'll talk more about it later. I know you have to get home."

"Yeah, I do, and thanks again."

"You're so welcome, sweetheart."

I waved, and I walked away almost in tears. The tears were from both from anxiety and excitement.

***

"Have you received an invitation yet?" Amber asked me as we walked out of class.

The invitation that she was talking about was for JaQuan's "All White Sweet Sixteen" birthday party this weekend. His invitation was a white envelope that would be hanging out from someone's lockers. The girls got white roses along with the envelope. From what I heard, no one knew when he would give the invitation because he wanted it to be a surprise, and it would hype up his party. But he would only give out invitations for three days. It was day three today.

"Nope," I replied.

"You may be getting one soon."

"It's almost the end of the day, so I doubt that he's gonna give me one."

"What happened to y'all though? You guys talked almost everyday a few weeks ago. Now y'all don't talk much."

Because I was threatening not to talk to him.

"We're just too busy."

We kept walking to our theater class when I noticed a large amount of people around the theater.

At this point, I was on ten. The more I walked through the crowd, the higher my anxiety was. The feeling of all eyes on me terrified me. I kept my head down and was still walking. I could hear snickers and whispers.

Are they talking about me?

Did Aryanna have something planned to humiliate me in front of the whole school?

Do I need to drop out?

Nope. Stop. Sit down and breathe.

I made it to the theater and took a seat. Now people were slowly gathering near me with their phones out.

OK. What's really going on?

Next thing I knew, someone handed me a white rose.

Wait. What?

Then, someone else handed me another rose. Then, another person handed me another white rose. I realized it was the Boy's Varsity Basketball team.

Oh, snap.

After the last player gave me the last rose, I looked around to find him. I looked behind me, and there he was wearing an all-white fit holding a bouquet of mixed white and red roses. Everyone was screaming and was recording everything. I looked around and realized that I saw Kay-Kay, Lauren, the twins, Mark, and Ty all video recording me and yelling for me. I put my hands on my mouth and put my head between my legs in shock.

Is this happening?

Is this really happening?

This is a dream. This has to be a dream, and I need to wake up.

I looked up, and it wasn't a dream. There he was in front of me. He looked as handsome as ever.

He flagged his hands down to have everyone to be quiet. Once the crowd was calm, he turned to me. "Hey, Starr," he said to me. "I know we haven't really talked in a while for whatever reason, but I wanted to say that I like you a lot, and I've been having fun hanging out with you."

"AAAAAWWWW!" the crowd exclaimed, causing me to blush.

"So, with that being said, since we have a Thursday game next week, I want to take you out on an official date next Friday."

"AAAAWWWWW."

"Annnndd not only are you invited to my party, but I would love for you to be my birthday date next Saturday."

I gasped, I grinned, and I gushed.

"So, what do you say?"

I hesitated a bit, but not too much. I wasn't even thinking about Aryanna, her crew, D-Rod, my anxiety or anything when I said, "Yes."

After that, everyone in the auditorium screamed when JaQuan gave me the roses and hugged me.

"OK, OK, kids." In came Ms. Bailey through the crowd. "She said yes, so if you don't belong in my class, you may exit the auditorium."

"I'll text you the details," JaQuan whispered in my ear. He let me go to give me a wink and left. I was so blushing and wanted to jump up and down, but I kept my composure.

My friends came up to me and quickly gave me a group hug. Kay-Kay and Lauren waved at me to go to class. I turned to Amber and playfully hit her shoulder and said, "You knew this whole time, and you set me up about it."

"I didn't set you up, I was trying to help you, friend," she whined and laughed. "At least you got a date with one of the popular guys in school

"OK, everyone, head to your seat," Ms. Bailey said. She walked up to me and whispered, "The flowers are beautiful." She gave a small smile and went to her desk.

I was barely paying attention for the rest of the class, as I held the roses and smelled them.

Chapter Eleven

"A DATE!" my mom yelled as we were getting the dinner table ready.

"Why are you yelling?"

"Because this is the first time you have been asked on a date. Oh, baby, I'm so happy for you!" She came over to me to give me a hug and kiss on the forehead.

"You have to tell me about this young man."

I told her his name and how he was a star basketball player, and about how he was an honor student. I even showed her a picture of him.

"Oh, he's handsome," she commented as she gave my phone back.

My daddy walked in and asked, "Who's handsome?"

Momma laughed and replied, "Someone in your daughter's class, who just asked her out on a date."

He stopped what he was doing. "A date?"

"Yes, someone asked our Starr on a date."

"Hold up." My dad pulled up a chair and started interrogating me about JaQuan.

What's his full name?

How old is he?

Where he's from

When is his birth date?

What's his social media?

What is his social security number?

That's when my mom butt in. "Darren! Leave that girl alone!"

"I'm asking our daughter some basic questions about this young man."

Momma chuckled. "You call those basic questions?"

"Yes. Yes they are."

She chuckled again and mumbled, "This man is crazy."

He turned his attention back to me. "Have you met his parents?"

"Not ye—"

"Great. Ask him if he and his parents can come over so we can meet them."

"Oh Lord, really, Darren?"

"What? Would you not want to check them out to see if they're not crazy?"

"Yeah, but you're really doing too much."

"No, I'm not. I need to check out this little boy who wants to take my baby on a date. If I see one red flag from either him or his parents, she can't go."

"Daaadddyy," I groaned.

"What? I'm so serious!"

"Momma, please stop him."

She chuckled and responded, "Listen, your daddy may be a little crazy, but he's looking out for you."

"So, that settles it. You can ask him if this Saturday at seven PM is good."

I moaned when I pulled out my phone and text him.

Me: Hey, my parents want to meet you and your parents on Saturday. Is that OK?

Momma called Skylar down and told her to bring Sekani, too.

"So, where is dinner? I'm starving," Daddy said.

As I was going to sit down in my chair, I received a notification on my phone. It was a text from JaQuan.

JaQuan: That's fine. What time, and my place or yours?

"Starr, what did we talk about phones during dinner?" Momma said sternly as she put Sekani in his seat.

"I know. It was JaQuan," I answered.

"Oh, what he said?"

"He asked what time, and are we having dinner at his or our house?"

"Here. At seven," Daddy answered.

Oh, God. He's gonna scare them away.

I regrettably text him back, and he responded quickly.

JaQuan: Sound great! My parents can't wait to meet you!

Now, I'm panicking.

***

The day of the dinner was here and I wasn't feeling it. I looked in my mirror to check myself out. I changed clothes I know at least six times. I decided to settle on a red cami dress. I had just started brushing my hair when my momma yelled, "Starr, come down and help me set the table."

I went down and set up the table with Momma and Skylar.

"Skylar, remember your manners, and be nice," Momma said.

"Yes ma'am," Skylar replied. "Will you be this extra when I get a boyfriend?"

"Oh, you won't be dating until you're thirty," Daddy answered the question as he walked by.

"Darren!" Momma yelled.

"What? I barely wanted Starr to date."

"You're doing too much now. What are you gonna do when Sekani starts to date?"

"He will be a ladies man when that happens. All the girls will love him."

"Now, wait a minute. How is it that he can date when he gets to high school, but the girls can't?"

"Because my girls are going to be independent, career women who won't need a man for anything."

"So, Sekani can't be independent and have a career too?"

They continued their debate when I walked up to Skylar to whisper, "Ignore him. He's being a daddy that doesn't want his girls to grow up."

Skylar muttered, "I know."

"Besides, if you bring a boy here, I'll do all the interrogating."

Skylar laughed.

She was laughing, but I was serious. I'd be an FBI agent when it came to Skylar and Sekani when they started dating. But it wouldn't happen for a few years. I waited in the living room feeling anxious when it got closer to seven o'clock.

What if his parents don't like them?

What if my parents don't like him or his parents?

What if something goes wrong?

My momma grabbed my hands. "Starr, you're panicking again."

I looked at her in confusion.

"What? What made you say that?" I asked her.

"You're looking into space and your breathing is off."

That's when I noticed that my breathing had sped up.

"Look, I know you may be nervous about meeting his parents, but everything will be OK. I promise nothing is gonna go wrong. I will make sure your daddy stays in line, too."

I chuckled when she gave me a forehead kiss. "I love you, Starr. I'm so proud of how far you've come."

"Thanks, and I love you too." Even after saying that, Aryanna and her bullying tactics still popped up in my head. It was at that moment that I wanted to tell her. I opened my mouth to say something when the doorbell rang. I quickly got up to open the door. I opened the door to see JaQuan wearing a white dress shirt, black dress pants, black dress shoes, and a black tie. He was also holding some flowers.

"Hey!" I said excitedly. Too excitedly to be honest.

"Hey," he replied back with a smile. "Here. These are for you." He handed me the flowers.

I was about to say something when Momma came to the door.

"Hey, JaQuan, I'm Mrs. Brown, Starr's mother."

"Hey, Mrs. Brown, it's nice to meet you."

Dad popped up at the door. "And I'm Mr. Brown, her daddy."

"How you doin', Mr. Brown? I'm JaQuan."

JaQuan held his hand out to give a handshake, and Daddy reached for it.

"So, JaQuan, where are your parents?" Momma questioned.

"Oh, here they come."

Coming from the corner was a beautiful-looking couple. His mother wore a long dress, looking like a supermodel, and his dad was definitely JaQuan's twin. JaQuan looked like his mom, and he got his dad's smiles.

"Oh, my God!" my mom yelled. I started to panic. *What's going on? What did they do?* "Sandra?" *Sandra?*

JaQuan's mom looked at my momma, and she looked shocked.

"Sunday?" Mrs. Watts said my momma's name.

Wait. They know each other.

"Oh, snap!" Mr. Watts exclaimed. "Darren?"

Yep, they know each other.

JaQuan's and my parents practically ran to each other to give each other a hug and we all came inside for dinner. Come to find out, they all graduated from Alabama A&T University together. My momma and Mrs. Watts are sorority sisters from the same line, and Mr. Watts was my dad's line dean from the same fraternity. They hadn't seen each other in over eighteen years since my parents moved to California.

After we finished dinner, JaQuan and I went outdoors, while Skylar and Sekani and our parents were in the dining room, catching up.

JaQuan sighed. "Well, that went well."

"I hope so," I replied.

JaQuan chuckled. "Come on, Starr. They like you."

I looked down at my fingers. "I guess."

"Starr. Look at me."

I looked up to him. *Oh, my God, you are so fine. Oh, God, I hope I didn't say that out loud.*

"My parents like you. Trust me, they are very picky of girls that I hang out with. They really feelin' you, especially my mom."

I smiled. "I guess you're right. My dad is *extremely* picky, but he's feeling you, too."

"I already know. You know, we got to work on your anxiety."

I quickly turned my head to him with questions coming in my head.

What? How? Who told him?

Maybe he was just talking.

"Yeah, I know you have anxiety."

I was stunned and was about to fumble my words when he said, "And before you say anything, let me explain. I kind of noticed how you don't like being in crowds, you don't talk to people for real, and you know what was really telling?"

I shook my head.

"When you become distant."

Distant… no.

"I kept wondering what I did to drive you away and make you not want to talk to me. I was really confused."

No, no, no, JaQuan. It's not you.

"So, I asked my cousin for some advice on what I should do. I told him about you, and he recognized that you might have anxiety because he got anxiety, too. Is he right?"

I slowly shook my head yes.

"Social anxiety," I replied to him in a low voice.

"Why didn't you tell me in the beginning?"

I was on the verge of tears, but he needed to know.

"I-I didn't know how to tell you. I didn't want anyone to know because at my last school everyone treated me like

I was a freak at the circus because I didn't talk to anyone or hang out with anyone. It's been like that from kindergarten to high school. That's part of the reason why we moved down here. To get away from the negativity. This was my chance to start over and be normal for once."

JaQuan grabbed my hands and turned to me. "Starr, nobody is normal. If I wanted someone normal, I would be bored for life. Nothing excites me to wake up in the morning anymore. Not even basketball. That's before I first saw you. When I saw you on the first day of school, the first thing I noticed was your smile and how it suddenly brightened up the classroom. I have been excited to go to first period ever since.

"I have been wanting to talk to you, but for some reason I couldn't come up to you because I was nervous and scared. That never happened to me before with any other girl."

We both laughed as tears run down my face.

"But, for real. When we talk, you made my day better and made me focus on the court. But, when you stopped talking to me, I was losing focus because I couldn't understand what went wrong, Now, I understand."

I looked down to hold back tears, but he lifted my head up to him. I didn't want to lie, but I didn't want to tell him about what happened at the game, so I just shrugged my shoulders.

"Starr, you don't have to have doubts about anything. That's why I ambushed you on that day in the auditorium because I knew if I would have given you a regular invitation, you would probably turn it down and maybe backed out. But, I wasn't having it."

I laughed and asked, "So, who's idea was it for you to pull that stunt on me in my theater class?"

He chuckled. "Actually, it was Ty's idea to do it there, and I was cool with Ms. Bailey. So, we figured why not there?"

"Yeah, it's official. I'm going to jump him."

"Hey, don't jump on him. At least you said yes to both invitations."

"I guess."

"But, I have a question for you."

"Sure."

"Is that why you never had a boyfriend before? Because they think you're weird?"

I nodded my head.

"That's unfortunate."

"Why do you say that?"

"Because they missed out on a beautiful person. I wouldn't care what anyone would say about you, you would definitely be mine."

My heart skipped a beat. It was like a magnetic force that was pulling our faces closer. I stopped mid-air because I was scared to go through with it. Even though I really wanted to.

JaQuan grabbed my hand and said, "Hey, it's OK. I got you."

Normally, I would turn away, but his eyes wouldn't let me. He leaned in more, and I closed my eyes and leaned in too. I could sense his lips were about to touch mine when suddenly we heard, "Hey, JaQuan, your momma said it's time to go!" Skylar yelled out.

He pulled back, looking annoyed. He yelled back, "Thanks, Skylar."

Yeah. Thanks, Skylar.

We got up to go inside to see our parents still laughing.

"We had a good time with you all," Mrs. Watts said, then she turned to me. "Starr, I really enjoyed you, and I'm very happy that my son met you."

I smiled at her.

"Thanks, Mrs. Watts."

Everyone hugged each other saying our goodbyes. When JaQuan got to me last, he whispered in my ear saying, "We'll have our first kiss soon." He pulled away and he gave me a wink before he walked out with his family. I was blushing as I waved at them.

When the door closed, my momma let out a huge sigh, "Well, that went better than I thought. Starr, come help me clean the table."

I nodded my head, and we started cleaning up. Daddy came to the room.

"Yeah, it's nice to see Sandra and Jayden again," my momma said.

"Yeah, it's crazy how small the world is," Daddy replied to Momma.

"Yeah, and they did a good job raising their son."

"Yeah, I actually like JaQuan."

Momma gasped. "Darren, did you just approve of this young man?"

"Hey, just because he's my frat's son, doesn't mean I automatically approve of him."

"Darren," Momma said in a stern voice.

"Fine." He turned to me. "Starr, I'm impressed by him. So, I approve of him."

I squealed, and I ran to hug him. I let go and he told me, "If he breaks your heart, I'll break his fingers, and he won't be able to play basketball for a while."

I wasn't stunting him because I was going on a date with JaQuan Watts.

Chapter Twelve

" *Remember that the Chess Club is going to be hosting a meeting next Tuesday, after school in Room 214,*" the morning announcer said over the intercom. *"Also, let's give a huge Wildcats congratulations to the football team on their big victory last night against the Holy Spring Patriots."*

The homeroom class cheered for the football team, especially for TJ and Jake. We won our Thursday game with a score of 45-42. It was a very intense game because both teams would score back-to-back. But, thanks to Jake, who blocked the defender from tackling their quarterback, our QB ran in for the touchdown with 1:10 left in the game. Then, it was TJ who made the interception that sealed the game.

After the morning announcement, Mr. Wright said, "Congratulations on the victory, TJ and Jake."

Jake replied, "Thanks, Mr. Wright."

"Now, it's time for you to be victorious in your presentation. Come on, boys."

We all chuckled as TJ and Jake got up. It didn't matter if you had a game the night before, you still had to do the presentation in Mr. Wright's class. The guys were chosen to do teen drunk driving. The guys were doing a mini skit. It was a serious topic, but they made it funny and relatable. With JaQuan a few seats in front of me, he would give me a quick glance with his beautiful smile. But, with Aryanna a few seats beside me, she would throw some paper ball at me just to bother me. She would do it when Mr. Wright wasn't looking because he would say something.

Once they got done, they gave their final analysis, Mr. Wright asked his questions, and they sat down. After the presentations, we just chilled and talked. I sat with my group of friends talking about the game, but I couldn't enjoy it because Aryanna got up to talk to her friends who were sitting beside me. While my friends were talking and laughing, I couldn't because I felt so uncomfortable with Aryanna next to me. Especially when I could clearly hear that they were talking about me, which was my biggest fear and could lead to a panic attack. But I managed to keep calm.

Then, they talked and laughed so loud. It was so annoying even Mr. Wright told them to tone it down.

Kay-Kay was giving a look that said, "*I'm gonna say something.*" I gave a look that said, "*Don't do it. It's not worth it.*"

I didn't want her to start anything with Aryanna. I didn't want anyone to get in trouble because of me.

"So, Starr," Lauren asked, "any idea where JaQuan is taking you tonight?"

I did not answer with Aryanna behind me, so I shrugged my shoulders. To be honest, I didn't know what we were gonna be doing tonight. He told me it was a surprise.

"Well, I know you'll be in good hands with JaQuan, and Kay-Kay and the twins are going to make you look good."

"You're not gonna help me get ready?"

Lauren sighed, "I wish I could, sis. But something came up, and I can't make it. But, please take pictures and put it in the group chat."

"It's OK. I understand, and we will."

BRRRRRIIIIINNNNNGGGG!

We all gathered our stuff and walked out the door. Suddenly, I felt a very hard bump from the back of my shoulder.

"My bad, Starr."

Aryanna.

She walked away with her friends, laughing. I just stood there until I felt something touch my shoulder, and I flinched a bit. I realized it was JaQuan.

"My bad, Starr," he said. "I was wondering if I could walk you to your next class?"

I took a quick look around and I answered, "Yeah, sure. That way, you can give me a hint on what we are doing tonight."

JaQuan laughed as we started walking.

"Just know that it'll be like a romance movie from back in the day."

"Oh, wow, that's all I'ma get? You're making this guessing game hard."

He put his arm around me. "Well, looks like you're gonna have to wait until tonight."

***

"BAM!" Ashley exclaimed after putting on my lashes. "Starr, you look gorgeous!"

I turned to look in the mirror, and I looked like a different person.

"Oh, snap," I responded.

"You look amazing, Starr."

"Oh, my God! I love it, Ashley!"

I really got some of the best of friends. Amber curled my sew in, Kay-Kay picked out my outfit, which was a black corduroy-overalls dress with a white, long-sleeve tank top and black and white Converses, and Ashley beat my face to high heaven. Ashley went to the door to tell everyone to come in to see the final result. I just kept looking at myself in the mirror. This was the first time that I felt beautiful.

My momma, Skylar, Amber, and Kay-Kay came in and were in awe.

"Oh, my God, Starr!" Momma exclaimed. "You look absolutely beautiful!"

"Yasss, cousin! I love it!" Kay-Kay approved.

"Starr, you look so pretty!" Amber complimented. "You look like something out of the *Black Teen Magazine*."

I didn't know about all that, but I'd take it. Everyone admired me for a few minutes then Kay-Kay and the twins left to do their own plans. After they left, I got back to see myself in the mirror. I needed to savor the moment. It was a rare occasion that I took selfies. But I looked too good to not take this. I took some pics, even a video, and posted it on the Gram.

After I made my post, I looked up at the mirror and realized that Skylar was standing in the hallway, looking at me.

"Hey, Skylar," I turned and greeted.

"Hey, Starr," she replied.

"What's wrong? Is he outside?" I panicked.

Skylar chuckled, "No, he is not out there yet."

"Oh, wassup then?"

Skylar entered my room. "You really look pretty, Starr."

I smiled.

"Thank you, Sky."

"I can't remember the last time that I saw you happy."

"Skylar, I was happy earlier."

"No, I meant, happy as in happy about life. Happy to be here. Happy as this is worth living."

I turned to her in shock at what she said.

Not going to lie. Back in LA, I thought about why I was here on Earth for me to be treated like that? I had even thought about leaving, but I couldn't leave Momma, Daddy, Skylar, and Sekani. So, I decided to write my feelings down in my diary and through my poems. Then, one day I accidentally left my diary open, and Skylar read it. Apparently, she went to Momma and asked her what suicide meant. That's how my parents found out about the bullying. I was eleven years old. The same age as Skylar is now.

"I'm fine, Skylar," I assured her. "I am happy."

"Are you sure?"

No. "I'm so sure, Sky. Give me a hug."

She came over and gave me a hug, and I almost cried on her shoulder.

We let go of each other and she asked, "Are you nervous?"

"Very," I chuckled.

"As fine as JaQuan is, I would be too."

I slapped her shoulder. "Girl, shut up."

"It's the truth! But it's OK, I don't want your man."

I chuckled. "Girl, please. I can't wait until you go on a date so I can clown you in front of your little boo."

"Oh, girl, whatever!"

We heard the doorbell ring, and we ran to my window to see Mr. Watts' car outside.

OMG, he's here.

I don't know if I can do this.

But I can't back out now.

What if I just say I've started not to feel well?

"Starr, you're breathing hard again. Get your emergency bag." Skylar snapped me back, and I could hear my wheezing breathing. I went to my drawer and grabbed my brown paper bag and took deep breaths with it.

Skylar rubbed my back. "Starr, I know you are nervous, but you need to calm down." After my breathing slowed down, my dad knocked on my door and announced, "Starr, your date is here."

I looked at Skylar, and I gave her a quick smile. I put my bag up and grabbed my purse.

I opened the door and said to Daddy, "I'm ready."

Chapter Thirteen

"What is this place?" I asked as we got out of the car and Mr. Watts drove off. We were currently in a city called Homewood, and we arrived at an arcade type of building with a sign that said *Blue Cave.* I looked up and noticed that it had people up there and loud music.

JaQuan responded, "This is a very low-key bowling alley for teens."

We walked inside, and it was so lit. Not only did they have bowling, but they had laser tag games, arcade games, and there was even a dance floor here.

"Hey, y'all, how can I help you this evening?" a blonde lady in front of us said.

JaQuan walked up to her and said, "Yes. Um, JaQuan Watts?"

She looked at the computer and looked up. "OK, your lane will be Lane 11 and should be ready in ten minutes."

"Thank you!"

"You're welcome. Y'all have fun."

"What do you want to do first before our lane is ready for us?" he asked me.

I sighed. "I don't know. It's too many options. What would you want to do?"

JaQuan searched the room and turned to me with a smile. "You like air hockey?"

***

"BOOM!" I yelled. We just finished our third round of bowling, which I won after it was tied up. So far, this date was everything I imagined my first date would be.

After we finished our bowling session and a few arcade games, we sat at a table nearby.

"Whew! That was fun," JaQuan said.

"Yeah," I replied. "Especially because I won."

"Oh, wow, you're not gonna let that go, are you?"

"Nope."

JaQuan laughed. "You're funny."

"I tried."

"So, how do you like West Park?"

Besides, Aryanna…

"It's good. I like it so far."

"That's good, and I noticed that you made a lot of friends quickly. I'm happy for you. Especially with what you went through."

"Thanks."

"It seems like you and Aryanna seem to be getting along, too."

TUH! No, we're not. She hates me, and I hate her. She's not even here and she is ruining the vibes of this date.

"We're just cordial."

"Hey, that's better than what most people at school are saying about her."

"What are they saying about her?"

"The fact that she is mean, rude, and downright evil."

All are true.

"But nobody really knows her. If only they knew what she went through."

I was intrigued. I cleared my throat. "Mind telling me what happened?"

"Well, her dad is currently in prison for attempted murder. I think he has about ten more years left. Her little brother was taken away by CPS because of the abuse that they both got from their mother. She was an alcoholic and violent. Her brother went with his father, and she went to her grandmother. Her brother was six years old, and she was eleven. She used to be the sweetest person who spoke up for people. But now, she's different."

Now, I felt bad. No wonder why she was so mean. But that didn't excuse her.

"You guys are good friends, huh?" I asked.

"Yeah, we were best buddies growing up. She and I used to do everything together until she moved."

I knew I shouldn't be, but I was a little jealous.

"Have you guys ever dated?" *Starr, why did you ask that?*

He chuckled. "Everyone keeps asking me that. No, we never dated, and we never will."

I sighed in relief.

"Besides, I'm here with you right now."

I blushed.

He grabbed my hand and told me to follow him. We went to the stairs that led into the nightclub-like dance floor with a DJ and some lights. He led me to the dance floor, and I held back.

"I don't do crowds. Plus, I can't dance."

JaQuan came up to me and said, "It's OK. Let's go over here."

He led us to a spot near the tables where no one was around.

"Is this OK?"

I shook my head yes.

JaQuan started doing his dance while rapping to a Drake song. I started to feel uncomfortable and started to look around to see if anyone was watching me.

"Hey." JaQuan used his hand to turn my head back to him. "Look at me. Don't worry about everyone else. Just focus on me."

He grabbed my hands and continued rapping. I calmed down and started rapping along with him. After a while, I started to loosen up and started dancing. It was the first time in a long time that I was actually having fun.

After a few more rap songs, the DJ got on the mic and said, "How is everyone doing out there?"

We all cheered.

"Alright, y'all, it's almost closing time. So, it's time for me to slow it down for all the young couples tonight. Can I do that?"

Everyone said, "Yeah," but me. *I actually have to slow dance with JaQuan?*

"All right, let's get lit."

The DJ started off with *Differences* by Ginuwine. I swallowed hard when he grabbed my hands and pulled me closer to him.

OMG, OMG, OMG. What if I step on his foot? What if he thinks I'm off beat?

"Hey," JaQuan snapped me out of my thoughts. "I can tell that you're nervous right now, but follow my lead. Put your arms around my neck."

I did as he told me, and he put his hands on my sides. My breathing picked up.

"Hey, I got you," he reassured me.

Breathe.

We swayed side to side with the beat of the music. I kept looking at my feet to make sure I didn't step on him.

"Starr, look at me."

I looked up at him and he looked deep in my eyes. I couldn't look away from him because he was so mesmerizing.

He leaned his head towards me and said, "I really enjoyed being with you."

"I enjoyed being with you, too," I replied without even thinking.

"I can tell we're gonna have so much fun with each other."

Heart, please be still.

"Really?" I asked.

"Yeah, I really enjoyed this date. Did you?"

"It's everything I imagined it to be."

He smiled and got closer to my lips.

OMG, this is it. My first ki—

"JaQuan!" someone yelled, interrupting us.

He looked up and said, "Oh, wassup man?"

Turns out the guy was JaQuan's teammate from AAU basketball when they were younger. They chatted for a bit, and the DJ announced that the Blue Cave was closed and he hoped to see us again.

The boys said their see-you-laters, and we started to make our way to the exit. I was more annoyed because this would've been a perfect first kiss, but this was the second time that we got interrupted. It made me wonder if this was a sign that we were not meant to be.

We got outside with the rest of the crowd. We were waiting on Mr. Watts, when JaQuan asked, "So, did you have a good time?"

"I did," I replied dryly.

"But?"

"There's no but."

"Something is bothering you."

"No, I'm fine.

JaQuan sighed. "You must be mad that we didn't have that kiss."

I looked at him and didn't say anything.

JaQuan smacked his lips. "Listen, I know that you wanted your first kiss to be perfect. I did too. It didn't look that way, but I was mad when my homeboy ruined our moment. But don't even front. We're going to have plenty of moments like that in the future. Especially tomorrow at my party. And you will be my guest of honor."

I honestly forgot about the party. Now, I had to figure out what I was going to wear.

"You're cool with that?"

I nodded my head.

"Good." He gave me a quick peck on the cheek.

OMG…He kissed me on the cheek.

JaQuan Watts actually kissed me on the cheek.

"Welp, there goes my dad."

Mr. Watts pulled up, and JaQuan opened the door for me like a gentleman. Then, we drove back to our side of town. Maybe tonight wasn't so bad after all.

Chapter Fourteen

"I don't know. I've changed my mind. I don't want to go." I panicked as I looked in the mirror.

Kay-Kay grabbed my shoulder and said in a panic, "No, no, no, no. We're not doing this."

"Kay-Kay, you don't understand. I can't do this. I just can't. What if something goes wrong?" I started to panic.

Kay-Kay immediately grabbed my emergency brown bag and had me breathing in and out. I calmed down after a few minutes.

"Now, listen," Kay-Kay whispered, "I know this is a lot right now and this is your first big party ever, but when you came here you asked me to help you overcome your anxiety, so you can have a good life here. That's what I intend to do, and this party is a huge step that could help you. But, if I see you panicking just once, I'm pulling you out."

I let out a sigh and nodded.

"Good. Now let's get you glammed up!"

Momma and Auntie Gina surprised me with a gorgeous dress for the party tonight. It was a one shoulder mini dress, with feathers on the one shoulder and a split. They even got me some clear heels. The plan was for me and the girls to get ready at my house and be there around 8 or 8:30 just so I could escort JaQuan to the party at 9 PM.

"Hey, girls, the twins and Lauren are here!" my momma yelled out.

"OK, they can come up!" I yelled back.

They came up, and they were admiring my makeup and hair.

"You look so gorgeous," Lauren complimented.

"Girlfriends better hold on to their boyfriends tonight," Ashley joked.

Amber turned to her twin. "Don't worry. She'll be too busy being with JaQuan to be thinking about any other boys."

"Speaking of with," Kay-Kay said, "how was your date with him?"

All the girls turned to me waiting on my answer.

"It was great." I told them that he was a gentleman the whole night and that we went to the Blue Cave, what games we played, and how we danced at the mini club on the roof.

"Did y'all kiss?" Amber was eager to ask that question.

"No, we didn't," I disappointedly answered.

"It's OK. It'll happen soon," Lauren assured.

I quietly replied, "Yeah, if."

"Uhn-uhn. When!" Lauren snapped. I was shocked that she even heard me.

"Yes ma'am," I replied.

"Hold on," Ashley jumped in. "While we were talking about Starr's date, what about your date, Lauren?"

The rest of us snapped our necks at Lauren.

"What date?" we all said in unison.

"Yesterday, I was hanging out with Mark—"

I turned to Ashley. "What are you doing with Mark?"

I remembered that Mark did tell me that he had a crush on Ashley.

"Girl, we were just hanging out. Anyways, me and Amber met up with Mark, Ty, TJ, and Jake at the movies and we saw a girl that looked mighty like Lauren. There was a guy that was with her that looked like Blue, and they were headed to see the new *Haunted Mansion* movie."

We turned to Lauren to look for some answer from her.

Lauren turned to Ashley. "You're such a tattletale."

"Why didn't you tell us you went out again? We won't judge you or anything."

"I know y'all wouldn't. It's just that I want to be sure."

"Sure, about what?"

"About everything. Like what will people say about me dating him? Besides all the trouble he got into last year, he's a sweet guy. He loves to read books, he loves to listen to old school R&B, he takes care of his grandma, who has a disability, and he volunteers at the community center after school."

Kay-Kay walked to her and said, "Oh, no, Lauren, you can't let people dictate who you should or shouldn't date. Sometimes, people judge a book by its cover, but that doesn't mean the story behind it is good or bad. Blue is a great guy, and I trust him to treat you right. But he got one time to mess up, and we'll mess up his life."

We all laughed because it was true. We all came up and hugged her. She then said, "I love you guys so much. But, can we get ready?"

"Yeah, I'm trying to find me a boo," Amber said.

I just laughed at my friends' conversation as they continued to get ready. But I took heed to what Kay-Kay said. I shouldn't worry about what people had to say about me and JaQuan. Only we could dictate that. Now I was ready to put on my dress.

***

"Hey, guys!" I said to our guy friends.

"Hey!" they all exclaimed as me and the girls walked into the party. The party was being held at a mansion that JaQuan's parents rented.

They all looked handsome with their white clothes. When I tell you, probably the whole school was here, and they didn't play about the theme. You didn't see any other color other than white. They all looked GOOD! The house was absolutely gorgeous! The all-white decorations were on point, too.

"You guys look good," Ty complimented us.

"Thanks, you guys do, too!" I responded.

Kiki Ellyse

"Well, we tried," TJ said, cockily.

I rolled my eyes and turned to Jake and Matt. "You look nice, Jake and Matt."

"Of course they look good," Ty jumped in. "They're white. It goes well with them."

"Man, don't be a hater," Matt replied. "The ladies still love it."

"That's right, Matt. Pop your stuff," Blue cheered.

"OK. OK. Respect." Ty dapped Matt up, then an NBA YoungBoy song came on, and we started to sing and dance.

Later on, more people came, and it was a struggle to try to hang on. But as long as I was with my friends, it kind of calmed me down. Even though I was still on high alert.

It was close to nine, and I had to meet with JaQuan outside to escort him in. As I made my way through the thick crowd, I accidentally bumped into someone, and it was D-Rod.

"Oh, I'm sorry," I said loudly over the music.

"It's OK, love," he responded as he was checking me out and licking his lips, making me uncomfortable.

"You look nice."

"Thanks," I said as I tried to move passed him, but he stopped me and said, "Where you goin', love?"

"I got to do something."

"Hold up, dance with me first."

"No, thanks, I got to go."

"Come on, it's only for a moment."

"Ay, man, leave her alone."

I turned, and it was Ty and Blue coming behind me.

D-Rod put his hands up and said, "Ayy, man, I don't want no trouble. Just trying to dance, that's all."

"Yeah, well, she said no," Blue said to him. He put his hands up and backed away, saying, "Respect. Respect."

I turned to Blue and Ty to thank them and then made my way outside. I looked around for JaQuan, and he was by the driveways. I almost melted as I got closer to him. He was

111

wearing his white suit with a gold necklace and freshly retwisted locs. He noticed me coming towards him, and his eyes widened. It made me wonder, *did I do something wrong?*

"Wow." He smiled. "You look beautiful."

I blushed as I gave him a hug.

"You look handsome, birthday boy," I complimented back.

"Yeah, you look really good. Like you look like you got out of a photoshoot."

"Thank you."

"You're welcome."

JaQuan looked to see if anyone was around before he turned back to me and started leaning in on my lips.

"You ready, kiddos?" Mr. Watts interrupted us.

Every time.

JaQuan quickly hid his annoyance and said, "Yeah, we're ready, Pops."

"Alright, let's go."

JaQuan turned to me.

"I'm sorry. I thought I could give you a quick kiss before we go in."

I sighed. "It's OK. I'm going to have a breakdown either way."

"If you do, I will take you away in a quiet space until you calm down. But, I think you're going to be OK."

"I hope so." I wrapped my arm around his arm, and we started to walk to the door. He gave me sunglasses.

I looked at them, and he said, "It's for us when we walk in. Mainly for you."

I smiled because I knew what these were for. I put them on and let out a huge breath.

Starr, you can't back out, now. Don't black out.

Mrs. Watts got on the mic to get the party goers' attention.

"Hello, everyone! Thank you so much for coming out to celebrate our boy on his sixteenth birthday. I wish I could get on here and embarrass him with some stories for you…"

He shook his head as I laughed at him.

"But, we have to bring in the birthday boy. Alright, you guys get your phones ready because he and his date did not come to play. Make some noise for the man of the hour, JaQuan!"

We started walking in, and I held on to him tight.

He then whispered, "I got you."

We walked through the door with the entrance song, *HIM* by Big Yavo. We were walking with a bunch of people screaming and cheering for us. With people recording us with flashes, that made me so nervous. What if I fell? What if I tripped? What if I made JaQuan trip? I could mess up this walk.

But I saw Kay-Kay, Lauren, Mark, the twins, TJ, Jake, and Ty yelling for me, and that helped me to calm down. I was waving at my friends, and JaQuan was waving at them, too.

"Aren't they beautiful, ladies and gentlemen?"

The crowd continued to cheer for us as JaQuan helped me up to the stage with Mrs. Watts.

"Alright, alright, alright, now it's time to hear from the man himself. Everyone, give it up for Mr. JaQuan Watts!"

We all clapped and yelled for him. He hugged his mom and grabbed the mic.

"YOOOOOOO!"

"YOOOOOO!" the crowd responded.

"Thank you all for coming to my birthday party. I want to thank God for being here right now. He blessed me by giving me two wonderful parents, who are my best friends." He turned to his parents. "I love you guys, and I'm going to give you guys your flowers."

He grabbed two bouquets of white roses from one of his teammates and handed them to his parents. Everyone, including me, was in awe and clapped when they embraced each other. After they all hugged, he got back on the mic.

"Shoutout to my family. Y'all are my life, and I love you."

Mrs. Watts blew him a kiss.

"Also, a huge shoutout to my teammates! Y'all are the real MVPs from last season. We couldn't make it to the championship, but we will this year. Love you, boys."

The varsity team cheered and shouted.

"Shout out to the whole school, but I want to give a special shoutout to my beautiful date tonight."

Everyone turned to me and shouted out, "Awwwwwww!"

"Starr, you look absolutely amazing, and you are an incredible person. Thank you for being my escort for tonight."

Everyone applauded as I was standing there blushing and nervous at the same time. I didn't feel comfortable with all these eyes on me because I didn't know if they were in awe because I was pretty or in awe because they didn't like me. I wasn't trying to show it, so I just kept smiling.

"But, once again, thank you all for coming out, and let's turn up!"

He put the mic up and grabbed my hands to lead me off the stage.

"We can go find a place where you can be comfortable and dance," JaQuan suggested.

Now, or later.

"Actually, I'm fine going to where our friends are," I said.

JaQuan looked shocked. "You're sure?"

"Yeah."

"Alright, let's go."

We were all dancing throughout the party, and for the first time, probably in all my life, I was happy.

Then, his parents announced that there was a surprise outside. We all knew what the surprise was. The question was, what kind was it? JaQuan held my hands and led me outside as everyone in the party followed. In front of the house was a black 2023 Dodge Charger SXT. When he saw the car, he immediately went to his parents, hugging and thanking them. Everyone was recording as he got into his car for the first time. He waved for me to come over, and I got inside to look inside the beautiful car.

"How do you like it?" JaQuan asked me.

"I should be asking you that," I laughed. "But, it's really nice. I like it."

"Man, I can't wait to ride this bad boy with you being my passenger princess."

I started blushing. We stayed out for a little bit then we went inside. I told Lauren and Kay-Kay that I was going to the restroom. As I was washing my hands, the door opened, and I looked at the mirror, and my heart dropped at who I was looking at.

"Y'all looked real cute out there tonight," Aryanna said while drinking her red juice. She was wearing a white, one-shoulder bodycon dress with feathers.

I was shaking. How could I go from having a good time to being scared in a matter of seconds?

"Hey, Aryanna," I said, shakily. "What are you doing?"

"Contemplating whether I should throw this juice on you and ruin your night, or if I should spare you."

I wanted to run out of here, but she was blocking the door.

"What did I do to you for you to hate me like this?"

"I don't hate you, but I told you to leave JaQuan alone because he deserves so much better than you."

I was trying not to show any weakness, but she hurt me with her words.

She started to walk closer to me. "But, I've seen how happy JaQuan is with you for whatever reason, and that's one of my good friends. So, you can still see him, but just know, I'm still going to make your life at Avondale hell, and you better not tell him about it. You got that?"

Once she got in my face, I frantically shook my head. She jerked her hand with the juice towards me, and I closed my eyes. I slowly opened my eyes and saw her smiling and laughing. I looked down and realized she didn't throw the juice on me, and she walked out.

"So scary," she chuckled.

I was starting to hyperventilate and cry. I immediately rushed out and headed outside when I bumped into Ty.

"Starr, are you—"

I didn't let him finish because I was just trying to go outside.

I made it to the backyard and practiced my breathing techniques.

Breathe through your lips as if you are whistling.
Slow your breathing to one breath every five seconds.
Belly breathing.

I could feel myself calming down, and I was admiring the pool when I heard my name behind me. It was JaQuan.

"Hey, you OK?"

I quickly fixed my dress to turned to him and replied back saying, "Yeah, I'm good. Just needed some fresh air."

"I'm sorry, I should've been with you."

"What do you mean?"

"I should've been with you and helped you outside. I know being around people can be too much."

I just played along.

"It was kind of too much, but I'm alright, seriously."

JaQuan sighed. "Good. Look, I didn't mean to catch you off guard, but I need to do this before we get interrupted again."

"Do what?"

He crushed his lips into mine. I was shocked, but a second later, I just naturally kissed him back.

O....M....G. I just got my first kiss.

Not just a regular first kiss. But my first kiss with JaQuan Watts.

He pulled back and he said something, but I was too focused on how soft and warm his lips were. That kiss was everything that I always dreamt of and more.

"Starr?"

I snapped out of it.

"Yeah?" I responded.

"You OK?"

"Yeah, yeah. I am."

No, you're not. You are literally screaming in your head.

"Was it good?"

"Yeah."

"Good, I would ask if we can kiss again, but if we stay here, we'll probably get interrupted again. But I'll give you another one when I take you home."

"OK," I said, grinning.

"We should get back to the party."

"Yeah, we should."

We headed back to the party, holding hands, smiling. This night was a roller coaster. This was the best and the scariest night of my life. I couldn't wait to tell my friends that I had my first kiss with JaQuan Watts.

Chapter Fifteen

"Great job in practice, ladies," Ms. Kennedy said to us as we stood around her at the end of practice. "This is homecoming, so you already know that our cheer alumni will be here, so be sure to show up and show out. Also, Riley has a fever of 103 degrees, so she won't be able to cheer tomorrow. Which means that Starr will be cheering with us tomorrow."

I stood there in shock as the whole squad screamed and ran to hug me. I felt excitement, nervousness, scared, and happy all in one moment. I was cheering in my first football game tomorrow. After Ms. Kennedy talked about the details for tomorrow, we were dismissed from practice, and I immediately called my parents.

***

"I can't believe that you're going to be cheering on the sideline, and I'll be dancing on the stand," Kay-Kay squealed.

Tonight, Lauren, Kay-Kay, the twins, and I decided to have a sleepover at Kay-Kay's house tonight and tomorrow night after the game. We were all sitting in her room eating pizza and some candy.

"Yeah, I'm so excited but scared at the same," I admitted.

"It's OK," Ashley said. "First game jitters are normal."

"Yeah," Kay-Kay jumped in. "I remember my first game last year. I was the only freshman on the dance line. I was scared out of my mind. I was crying, feeling I was about to throw up. But, when I marched in for the first time and saw my family and friends cheering for me, all of that went away, and I danced like I was a vet."

"I remember that game, too," Amber said. "We got beat severely by J.O."

"Oh, yeah, it was like 42-7 I think." Lauren chuckled.

Kay-Kay laughed. "I remember. I'm sitting there on the benches like 'Oh, my God, can Mr. Woods play some music so we can make the game somewhat interesting?'"

We all laughed.

"No, do you guys remember when that guy got jumped?" Amber asked.

"Wait, hold up, who got jumped?" I curiously asked.

"Basically, we played against East Lake, and this boy that went to our side was talking so much crap. Then, he decided to mess with some boys that went to our school who are known to fight anyone. Next thing you know, the boy got into one of the other boy's faces and pushed him, and they all pounced on him."

I started laughing.

"Hold on, I found the video," Lauren said.

We all gathered around her and watched the video. We all laughed as the boy was mocking him, and the Avondale guys were ignoring him, and the boy pushed one of the Avondale guys, and they all went in on him. By the time they broke up, the other guy was a mess. His clothes were messed up, he could barely walk, and he got some blood on his shirt.

Lauren shook her head. "I don't condone violence, but he was asking for it."

"I'm trying to figure out why he would come to the visitor's side and want to start trouble?" Amber asked.

"I mean, it is East Lake," Ashley said.

"Yeah, they are weird over there."

They continued to talk while I felt a little inspired, so I pulled out my notebook and pen and started writing

Black Girls deserves joy,
We want representation in our toys,

We want respect from the boys,
We are Queens,
Stop labeling us as mean,
We deserve to be on the TV screen,
Not to be a bitter baby mama,
Not to be full of drama,
And not full of trauma.
We deserve to see us as rich material girls,
Astronauts, Chiefs, Models, Explorers, Cowgirls,
We want to see more of our bouncing curls,
Our stories don't have to be tragic,
It doesn't have to be ratchet,
Let's show our Black Girl Magic,
We deserve respect from boys,
We deserve representation in our toys,
Black Girls deserve joy.

"What you over there writing about?" Kay-Kay asked as I was finishing up.

"A poem," I responded.

"Can we see?"

I never showed anyone my work because I was scared of the reaction, but these were my friends, so I knew they would like it. I handed them my journal, and they all gathered around to read it. The silence made me so anxious. Then, Amber looked up at me and said, "I love it!"

I quietly let out a sigh of relief.

"Yeah, you got talent," Ashley agreed.

"It's just something to do." I shrugged.

"You should show the world your talent," Lauren said. "Have you ever thought about songwriting?"

"Noooo," I laughed. "I could never be a songwriter. I only write poems."

"Rap songs are like poems. You should definitely do it. You need to enter the *Black Teen Magazine* contest."

I'd never seen myself as a songwriter. I figured I could be an English teacher and just write poems for my collection. It could be a great career for me, and I wouldn't be in the spotlight. But I still had doubts.

"I don't know, y'all. There are other writers that are way more talented than me."

"You are just as talented as them," Kay-Kay complimented. "I know I'm overstepping my boundary, but I'm reading your other works now, and you got it. But we need you to open up more."

"What if I don't win, and nobody supports me?"

"Not true," Ashley said. "I'll watch it. Amber will be watching. Lauren will be watching. You know Kay-Kay will be watching. Your family will be watching. The guys will be watching. JaQuan will definitely be supporting his lil' boo thang."

Amber and Kay-Kay went, "Ouuuuuu."

I felt my cheeks going red.

"And I know you will, but what if I don't get noticed there?"

"See how she didn't deny being his boo thang?"

"Mhhhmmmm," Amber and Kay-Kay said in unison.

I chuckled. "Listen, I appreciate you guys' support, but I don't know if this is for me."

"Just think about it. Never know unless you try, Starr."

Maybe they're right. Maybe it's my calling, or this would be one of my rejects. Never know until I try.

***

"Great job, Starr!" Kourtney said as we walked out of the game. "We might need you for the next game."

We just finished cheerleading at the homecoming game, and it was amazing. I got the chance to cheer at my first football game ever. I even started tumbling, and the crowd loved it.

They even came up to Ms. Kennedy to ask where I was the whole season. I saw all my friends and family yelling for me. Even JaQuan and his parents were there to support me. It was a great experience until Aryanna and her minions walked in and changed the atmosphere. She even went over to where JaQuan and his parents were and started chatting with them, making me feel some type of way. I knew she was doing it on purpose to try to spike me, and it was working. But I couldn't let it show. I kept the smile on my face, and I caught her looking straight at me and started laughing.

I kept my cool and let it ride for the entire game. We ended up winning 45-17 against Parker. TJ and Jake came by and gave me a big hug between the both of them. After the game, my friend was talking about hanging at the tailgate to see what was going on over there, but I didn't feel too comfortable with the crowd, so I stood at the gate when I heard, "Great job out there." I turned to see it was Aryanna, which made my stomach sick. "Especially with you taking my spot and all."

"You quit, remember?" I snapped back a bit. I could feel the nervousness in my voice. "I've earned this spot."

Aryanna turned to her friends and chuckled, "Oh, she got a little bold, didn't she?"

I swallowed.

"She ain't gonna do nothin'," Katrina chimed in.

"Oh, I know she can't." She turned to me. "She's not about it, are you, Starr?"

I wanted to tell her off so badly, but I knew if I fought her, she would find a way to get on me, and I would get in trouble. Then, on top of that, I was still in my cheer uniform. I could get kicked out of the squad after my very first game. So, I just stood there, not saying anything. Like an idiot.

Aryanna smirked. "Thought so."

She walked past me and bumped my shoulder, and Rayanna and Katrina laughed, walking behind her. I felt nothing but anger inside me. I was madder at myself because I shouldn't speak out, but I couldn't.

"Girl, get your butt in the car, thinking that you're cute in front of your friends." I heard a woman's voice behind me.

I turned to the gate, and I saw Aryanna turn to her friends to tell them bye, and she got into the car. I heard yelling even after they drove off. That must have been her momma.

"Did good out there."

I got startled, and I turned to see it was JaQuan.

We both laughed.

"Dude, you don't sneak behind black people like that. That's how people get shot."

"You don't even own a gun."

"Boy, you don't know what I got."

"I know you have a pretty face, a pretty smile, and a pretty big forehead."

I could feel my face going red.

"Other than that, you don't know what I got."

He chuckled. "You're so silly." He gave me a peck on the cheek.

"You're not going to the tailgate?"

"No," I answered. "It's too many people, and I'm waiting for my friends and family."

"Do you need company?"

"You don't want to hang out with your friends?"

"They won't miss me. Besides, I would rather hang with you."

His words made me smile.

"OK."

***

"Girl, sit still," Amber told Lauren.

"I would, but you are literally yanking my hair," Lauren complained. Amber was giving Lauren big butterfly box braids. We were all back in Kay-Kay's room after the game.

"That's because you're so tender-headed. I was trying to make you look nice for your date tomorrow."

"I don't get the big deal. It's only Blue."

"It's only Blue, but you like him."

Lauren smirked because she knew it was true.

"He's cool."

"Just cool?" Ashley yelled out. "You two were practically inseparable at that game."

"OK, I might be feeling him just a little bit."

"Girl—" Ashley playfully hit her with a pillow.

"Aye, be careful, I'm still braiding here." Amber reminded her twin.

They were all continuing to talk and giving the latest school gossip, and I kept thinking about Aryanna and her mom. I couldn't help but to wonder what it was like for her.

"Hey, y'all," I spoke up. "Has Aryanna always been so mean?"

It was silence at first, then, Kay-Kay replied, "No, she wasn't. She was sweet, and kind, and we all were friends at one point. Until her dad went to prison and her momma went crazy. She became so distant and wasn't talking to us at all. But, when her and her brother went to live with his grandmother, she came around more and became friends with us again. Everything was good, until she got to middle school, and she went back to live with her momma again."

"What happened?"

"She decided in the seventh grade to hang with the older crowd and started to rebel. We were all still friends with her even after other people told us not to be. Then, one day she told me that Amber and Ashley were talking about me and

Lauren behind our backs. Then, the very next day, when we got to school, the twins came to us, wanting to fight."

Amber burst out laughing. "In our defense, she told us that y'all was planning on jumping us."

"She told us that y'all said that we were ugly and not about that life and was planning on fighting us." Lauren jumped in.

Kay-Kay then said, "And we had been planning for them to do something, but we didn't expect for them to do it the next day. So, after a bit of arguing that put us in the principal's office and put us in after school detention, we found out that Aryanna had made everything up to start drama."

I shook my head. "That's messed up."

"What's even more messed up is when we confronted her about it, she admitted to it and when we asked her why, she shrugged her shoulders and said because she was bored. We cut her off from our group, and we had beef since."

"Do you think it's her momma that had her acting this way?"

"That's part of the reason. But she definitely has issues."

Now that I saw the root of her issues, I could give her the benefit of the doubt.

"Maybe one day, we can all squash it together," I suggested.

Amber chuckled. "That'll be a cold day in Hades."

"Hey, you never know. Maybe, one day, we can help her, and we can all be friends."

Maybe.

Chapter Sixteen

These past couple of weeks had been a roller coaster. The football team made the playoffs, and we got to round two before we lost to Jasper. Around the same time, I was working on my poem to enter the contest, working with the poetry club, and on top of that, it was basketball season! So, our schedule was hectic, so JaQuan and I hadn't been hanging out as much. But the varsity cheerleaders rode with the basketball varsity team on away games, and we saw each other during home games, so we chatted a bit before the games.

It was the Friday home game before our Thanksgiving break. Then after the break would be the annual Winter Wonderland Ball. It was a dance that the school had that helped raise money for the Ronald McDonald House to help give the children presents for Christmas. Everyone in our group was going to the dance with a date but me. I mean, everyone expect me and JaQuan to went together, but he hadn't asked me yet, and I wasn't about to ask him. But I knew he would, hopefully.

We were currently tied 56-56 with 2:12 minutes left in the game against Carven, and we were in timeout. The Carven cheerleaders tried to do a diss cheer against us.

You want to talk?
You wanna run your mouth?
You want Craven to turn up in your house,
We'll set this gym off,
Set this gym off,
We'll set this gym off,
Set this gym off,
Set! This! Gym! Off!

They thought they did that, but we had a comeback cheer for them.

"You ready?" Ms. Kennedy asked me.

"Yep," I said with so much confidence to hide my nervousness. I got up from the bleachers and got into my position on the floor.

We're gonna be honest, don't get mad,
But that cheer you did makes you look bad,
We are the best team around,
Everyone knows that Craven is the joke of the town,
You're known for being clowns,
We're known for not backing down,
How you guys trying to rumble,
When you can't even tumble?

That was my cue to run out and put my all-star experience to use.

Roundoff, back handspring, back handspring, back handspring, tuck, roundoff, back handspring, back handspring, and a full twist twisting layout.

After I stuck the landing, I got up, and the whole gym was on their feet cheering for me. I looked at the Craven cheerleaders, and they looked maaaaadd.

I ran back to my teammates, and they were cheering me on.

"Great job, girlie," Ms. Kennedy said as she hugged me.

That excitement was everything the crowd needed to hype up the team. It was still a back-and-forth game before a Craven player bumped into JaQuan hard when he tried to shoot a three. The ref called a foul, and JaQuan could shoot three free throws with only 0:05 seconds left. The girls pushed me out to the jump line because they thought we were dating. I went out anyway for him even though we weren't official.

As JaQuan was in his shooting stance on the free throw line, Craven was making noise to throw him off, but it didn't work.

Swish.
Toe Touch.
57-58

The ref gave JaQuan back the ball. Craven was telling him to miss it. But he didn't listen.

Swish.
Another Toe Touch.
58-58.

If he made the next throw, we would win. If not, overtime.

JaQuan got to his shooting stance, and Craven was the loudest that they had ever been all night, only for that to fail.

Swish.
Toe Touch, back handspring. Just for him.
59-58.

After the buzzer sounded, the Avondale crowd went to the court and surrounded him to lift JaQuan in the air. I wanted to run up and give him a big hug, but I couldn't. I couldn't force myself to go in that crowd, but I was sure he'd understand.

A few minutes later, after I packed up my bag, a whole group of people came inside the gym and were coming towards me. I was about to panic until I saw all my friends holding their phones.

OMG. I think I know what this is.

Just as I predicted, JaQuan came in with red heart balloons, red roses, a teddy bear, and a poster. I hid my face with my hands in nervousness. I couldn't believe this was happening again.

Everyone was screaming and cheering for us. I felt his presence next to me, and I could read the sign:

Will You Cheer Me Up By Going To The Winter Wonderland Dance With Me?

It was so cute, and I looked up at him and he asked me, "Well, what say you, beautiful?"

He already knew my answer.

***

"Ouuuu, purple would be gorgeous on them," Mrs. Watts said to my mama as they looked for dresses and suits for the dance. It was Thanksgiving Day, and we decided to join the Watts after we left our family Thanksgiving dinner.

As our mothers searched and our father were watching the football game, JaQuan, Skylar, Sekani, and I were playing Uno in the living room.

"OK, Sekani, you can pull this card," Skylar instructed Sekani as she held his cards for him. He pulled the card and started playing with it.

JaQuan and I both laughed as Skylar pulled the card for him.

"I don't think he understands the game, Sky," I chuckled.

"Nuh-uhn," Skylar replied. "If he can operate a phone, he can play UNO."

We laughed again. After five rounds of UNO, which Sekani won two of them and JaQuan won three, we decided to go outside to the cool air and play some rounds of basketball on the court in the Watts' backyard. It was fun to watch JaQuan teaching Skylar the fundamentals of basketball. But, seeing them actually playing with each other, made my heart feel warm. Sekani got antsy because he wanted to play, so JaQuan gave him the ball and picked him up to put it through the basket. I could tell from his laughter that Sekani liked JaQuan.

After ten minutes, JaQuan and I took a break and sat at the patio table, and Skylar took Sekani in to go to the bathroom.

"You seem like you could be a great big brother," I said to him,

"Yeah," he said as he took a sip of water. "It would be nice to have some siblings in the house."

"You can have mine," I joked.

He chuckled. "Dang, you want to get rid of them that bad?"

"No, I'm playing. They're my heart."

"I hope one day that you'll let me in."

I was taken back on what he said.

"Why do you always have something romantic to say?"

"I'm a romantic. That's why."

"I bet you do this to all the girls in school."

"Not really, because all the girls are not like you."

I blushed so hard that my cheeks turned red.

JaQuan licked his lips and leaned towards me.

"No," I whispered. "What if someone walked in on us?"

"You don't see anyone coming do you?"

I looked out the window, and I saw our dads still watching the game, and I didn't see our mommas or my siblings.

I shook my head.

"Then, we should make it quick."

JaQuan leaned in, and our lips met. This felt like our first kiss all over again. The warmth and sensation had me in another world that I didn't want to leave.

"Starr! JaQuan!" We both jumped away when hearing my momma's voice come from inside the house.

"Ma'am?" I yelled out.

"Y'all come in and look at the outfits we found!"

JaQuan sighed and shook his head, and I laughed as we went inside.

***

"OK, turn around," Momma told me. I turned to the mirror, and I was amazed. This purple ruched, sequin bodycon dress had me looking like one of the Instagram models, thanks to Momma and Mrs. Watts. My body wave hair slayed thanks to Ashley. My make-up was on point, thanks to Kay-Kay.

"I look beautiful." I admired myself. That was the first time ever that I said that I was beautiful.

"You've always been beautiful," Kay-Kay said. "You just have to tell yourself that everyday."

The girls looked good, too. Kay-Kay wore a royal-blue long dress, Lauren wore a long, black sequin dress, and the twins wore matching sequin dresses ,with Amber wearing red and Ashley wearing gold.

I turned to them.

"Thank you," I choked up. "Thank you, guys, for everything. I love you guys so much."

The girls "awed" and came to me for a group hug. This would be so uncomfortable, but they made it so easy for me.

"Alright, alright, let's go before we mess up our makeup." Amber chuckled.

"Thank you, girls, for being friends with our Starr," Momma chimed in.

"Starr is a sweet person," Lauren told my mom as she looked at me smiling.

"So are you, pretty girls."

We could hear the door open and voices.

"Sounds like your dates are here," Momma announced. "I'll just let them know that you all are about ready."

As my momma went downstairs, we gathered our stuff and did our final touch up. I took one last look in the mirror when Kay-Kay came right beside me to start taking pictures on her phone, and I posed for the camera.

"You know what I've noticed?" Kay-Kay question.

"What?" I replied.

"You haven't been freaking out lately."

I smirked at her and said, "Don't get me wrong. I'm still as nervous as ever. I feel like I might throw up. But I know it's all in my mind, and that was holding me back after all these years. But, because of you guys and JaQuan, I've been happy, and I'm not going to let it stop me from having fun or having a life."

Kay-Kay didn't say anything—she just hugged me. "I love you, Starr."

I hugged her back. "I love you, too, Kayla."

"Now you just ruined the moment. I told you about using my first name."

We both laughed because she knew that I would forever call her Kayla, and I was the only one who could get away with it.

"Let's go, the boys are waiting on us."

"Wow." JaQuan was stunned as I came down the stairs. "You look beautiful."

He looked as handsome as ever with his purple suit and his freshly retwisted locs.

"Thank you." I grinned.

Everyone looked good. Lauren is going with Blue, Kay-Kay went with TJ, Jake was bringing in his girlfriend that went to a different school, Ashley and Amber were going with some of JaQuan's teammates, Joel and Richie, and Mark was going alone. I felt bad for him. I'd tried to convince him to ask Ashley, but he didn't because he was scared of rejection.

We all rode in a limo thanks to Mr. Watts and pulled up to the school in style. The gym was literally a winter wonderland. All the decorations were snowy white and snowflakes hanging from the ceiling.

"The committee did an excellent job with this," I admired the gym. "It's beautiful."

"Not as beautiful as you," JaQuan complimented me.

I just rolled my eyes. "You know that you always say that, right? I know I'm beautiful right now."

"But you're beautiful every day, and I'm here to remind you of that. Even without the pretty dresses and the make-up, it doesn't change the fact that I think you're beautiful."

I smiled at him, and as I was about to lean toward him to give him a kiss, Ashley rushed over to us.

"Hey, we're about to take some pictures at the background drop."

I nodded my head, hiding my annoyance.

JaQuan peeped it, laughed, and pulled my arm to go to our friends. After we took a couple of pictures, we went to the dance floor. Then, Ty came and joined us. Everyone in our group almost fell on each other trying to get to him. He had always been the light in our group with his smile. Whenever one of us had a bad day, he would make sure that you felt better; whether he was making jokes or playing one of your favorite songs. So now that everyone was here, the party could really begin. The playlist that the DJ was playing was making the whole gym jump.

Then, Mark and Jake decided to have a white boy dance battle. It was fun and funny to watch because both of them had no rhythm. We did a couple of dancing slides before the DJ slowed the music down for the couple. JaQuan found me in the crowd and held his hand out to invite me to dance. I gave a quick look at my excited friends, and I gladly took his hand, and we began to slow dance.

"Are you OK?" JaQuan asked in concern.

"I'm fine, seriously," I assured him.

"I'm asking just to be sure if you want to move away from the crowd."

"No, I'm fine. As long as you're here."

My words gave him the biggest, most beautiful smile I'd seen.

I was just lost in his pretty, dark brown eyes when he said, "Starr?"

I snapped back into reality.

"Yeah?"

"I know we have been talking for a minute and been hanging out for a little bit. But I really, really like you, and I enjoy being around you. I was wondering if you want to make us official as boyfriend and girlfriend?"

Starr, breathe before you pass out.

But I could not believe it.

A few months ago, I wouldn't even talk to a guy that I liked, and I couldn't look in his eyes. But now, I was dancing with the guy of my dreams, and he asked me, ME, to be his girlfriend. I wasn't thinking about anything when I responded back saying, "Yes, yes I would."

He quickly picked me up and spun me around, and he hugged me. I looked around and saw everyone around us looking at us funny. I was laughing because it was cute and embarrassing.

"You're pretty excited for someone who just asked someone to be their girlfriend."

"You have no idea how nervous I was asking you."

"Why would I say no?"

He whispered to my ears, "Because of your anxiety. I was hoping it wouldn't make you second guess us."

I looked at him and told him, "No, I wouldn't say no. I was worried that you wanted to stay friends. Even though there's nothing wrong with us being friends. Yeah, I'll probably be disappointed—"

He cut me off by kissing me again. Every doubt I had in me was gone, and I kissed him back. His soft lips were so heavenly. I could see what it was like to kiss your crush in teen movies.

JaQuan pulled back and asked, "Is that something that friends do?"

I wanted to say some of them did, but I shook my head, saying, "No."

"Alright then, then it's official. You're my girl and I'm your boyfriend."

I started cheesing. "OK."

*AHHHHHHHHHHHHHHHHHHHHHHHHHHHHHHHHH
HHHHHHHHHHHHHHHHHHHHHHHHHHHHHHHHHHHH*
.

*OMG.   OK,   Starr,   deep   breaths.
AHHHHHHHHHHHHHHHHHHHHH.*

I can't believe it.

*I can't believe that I finally got a boyfriend. Not just any
boy, but JaQuan Watts.*

*I can't wait to tell my momma so she can tell my daddy.
So, I won't do it. But the girls are gonna freak.*

After a few more slow dances and kisses, I excused
myself to go to the restroom to freshen myself up. After
reapplying my lip gloss, the door flung open, and Rayanna,
wearing a green dress with a yellow lace front, Katrina,
wearing an orange dress with burnt orange hair, and Aryanna
with a hot red dress with a high split with long black straight
hair, walked in. A perfectly good night quickly ended by the
sight of them.

"Hey, S-S-S-Starr," Aryanna mocked me. "I hope
you're having fun with JaQuan, even though you don't
deserve him."

I swallowed hard, but I couldn't be scared anymore.

"What's your issue with me, Aryanna?"

Aryanna laughed.

"I have no issue with you. Just don't see the big deal
with you."

I had enough of this.

"Look, I have no issue with you, OK? I'm not trying to
take your place in this school. If you want to be the queen of
the school, fine. Take it. I don't want it. I honestly feel sorry
for you. I know about your falling out with Kay-Kay,
Lauren, and the twins. I understand that your mom was h—"

SMACK!

Before I could respond to the slap on my cheek, she
grabbed my hair and basically threw me to the wall, and I
fell to the ground. She walked up to me to kick me in the

stomach. I had no time to process my pain when she walked over to me to grab my hair and made me look at her.

"You don't know nothing about me or my momma. Those girls got no business telling you about me. Now, I'm on ten. See, I was going easy on you and let you slide. But now, I'm going to make you and all your friends' lives here hell. All thanks to you for thinking that you can step up to me and run your mouth. So, when they ask me why I'm doing what I'm finna do, I'm gonna say 'Ask Starr' and that'll be a good reason for nobody to talk to you."

She let go of my hair, and they left the restroom.

I was laying on the restroom floor sobbing in pain. I'd never seen anyone so angry with anything. At that moment, it was almost like I was looking at the devil. I used the sink to help me slowly get up, and I looked in the mirror. I looked horrible with my makeup smeared and my hair mess up. I was still crying as I was doing my best to fix myself up. I couldn't believe that someone had that much anger inside them.

After I straightened myself up the best way I could, I left the restroom, and I ran outside to get some air before I passed out.

I'm knelling down to try to catch my breath and on the verge of tears. After I calm down and start breathing right, I feel like I have to go. As I'm was about to go back inside and tell JaQuan that I want to go home, I turned around and I got startled from someone that standing behind me.

Lauren.

"You OK?" she asked.

Does she notice anything off about me? Did I do a bad job of hiding it?"

"No," I lied.

"Oh OK we've been waiting for you to come back so we can do the Tamia line."

"OK. Here I come."

Thank goodness.

This night had gone from the best to the worst. I just wanted to go home and be away from people, but I didn't want to ruin anyone else's night. especially after what Aryanna said to me. I just hoped she wasn't serious about making our lives here miserable.

Chapter Seventeen

B ut Hell on earth was what she brought. With only a week left in school before our winter break, she caused chaos. There was a series of inappropriate drawings on people's lockers, including mine. But my locker was way worse than the rest. Seeing different, horrible name-calling and slurs made me sick to my stomach. Even when I was back in LA, it was never as bad as it is now.

Someone put a dead snake in Mark's bookbag, and that caused him to have a panic attack in the hallway. Mark was screaming and running all over the hallway. People were laughing at him, causing a commotion in the hallway. He had to go home early because of it. Only certain people knew about his fear of snakes. Then, someone went to the auditorium and made it a mess. Trash everywhere, spray paint on the wall, all of the art supplies were thrown on the stage curtains, and food condiments and food were all over the floor. It was the day that the poetry club was supposed to have a Christmas party.

What made matters worse was the Facebook page. Someone created an anonymous Facebook account and was exposing almost everyone at the school. From someone who was cheating with their best friend's girlfriend, to a known church girl being caught smoking, to smart kids using drugs to stay awake, etc. They would even comment on people's Facebook pages, harassing them. It was crazy.

"See, they posted something else," TJ said as he and Jake were walking me home.

Jake and I went to look at the phone, and it was another post from the page:

A little birdie told me that a baseball player is a little sweet 👀 🐸 🍵

"This is getting out of control," TJ said.

"Who is this behind the page?" Jake asked.

I was pretty sure that I had an idea of who it was, but I wasn't saying anything. Because she would label me as a snitch, which would ruin my high school status.

"Whoever this is needs to stay anonymous," TJ commented. "If word gets out who it is, they need to use their feet and run."

Jake laughed, "For sure, they'll be a track star that day."

I laughed along with them to make it unawkward for me. I finally made it home, and before I could go inside, I received a text from Kay-Kay:

Cuzzo/Bestie: SOS! My house. ASAP.

Oh no.

I started to run. TJ yelled out if I was OK, and I didn't respond to him. I just kept running until I made it to Kay-Kay's house. I burst into the door, and I was shocked by what I saw. Sitting on the couch was Amber with her hair all messed up, bloody nose, and bruises on her arms. Ashley was cleaning her face. I gasped, and I put my hands on my mouth.

"What happened to you, Amber?" I asked.

"That Facebook page posted a status about me having Bipolar Disorder saying I was suicidal. It said that I should've done it. That's when I knew."

"Knew what?"

"I knew that the person behind that page was Aryanna. Only Ashley, Lauren, Kay-Kay, and Aryanna knew about my mental illnesses.

"I've seen the post, and I've told her not to do anything," Ashley stated.

"I got so hot that I went looking for her after school without anyone noticing. I found her at the park with her minion and D-Rod. I confronted her, and she acted like she didn't know what I was talking about. She just started laughing, and I lost it. I had the upper hand until she kicked my knees, and that caused me to fall, and she ended up with the upper hands. I wasn't trying to fight her, but ugh! She made me stoop to her level."

"Amber, I'm sorry," I apologized to her.

"Why is she doing this?" Ashley asked. "We didn't do anything to her."

But I knew the reason.

"I don't know what her issue is, but she's tripping," Ka-Kay said. "I had a feeling that it was her, but we don't have proof that she's the one who made those posts."

"Why can't we go to Mr. Curry about what she did?" Ashley suggested.

"They're not gonna believe us. All she's gonna have to do is act all innocent and deny everything. It's going to be a she-say-she-say situation."

I just shook my head because I knew Kay-Kay was right. If there was no proof, she could get away with anything. She pretty much controlled us and the whole school.

"We'll find a way," Ashley responded.

The long silence was tense, and you could feel it.

"I'm sorry that I didn't tell you that I'm bipolar, Starr. I should've been honest to you about that," Amber said in a shaky voice.

I swallowed. "I-It's OK. I'm not mad. Here, I can fix your hair."

I couldn't tell them what Aryanna said to me at the dance because it would add fuel to the fire that I didn't want.

"Thanks." She started crying. "I love you guys so much."

I went up to her to give her a hug and started combing her hair, but I felt guilty.

Chapter Eighteen

This Christmas break was something that everyone needed. The anonymous page had slowed down and wasn't causing trouble. A lot of people were away for the holidays and spent time with their family. We went down to spend Christmas at both of my grandparents' houses. It was the first Christmas that I had spent in Alabama, and it was probably the best Christmas I ever had. We'd gotten more presents from our grandparents, I got to meet other family members, I got to know a few cousins that were in my age range on my dad's side, and we made a connection.

On New Year's Eve we decided to stay at home and invited the Watts family to our house to spend New Year's with us. Sekani refused to go to sleep, so he was with Skylar most of the night. We stayed up to play games, dance to the music, and had a mini karaoke until it was time for the countdown on the TV. JaQuan grabbed my hands and pulled me behind our parents because we planned to have our New Year's kiss, but we didn't want our parents to see.

"Three! Two! One! HAPPY NEW YEARS!" we all yelled.

As our parents were making a toast, we turned to each other and shared a quick peck and hug. After we let go, I saw Skylar with her mouth wide open, looking at us.

She saw us kissing.

I put my finger on my lips, telling her to not say anything.

She mouthed, "You owe me."

I rolled my eyes. She got on my nerves, but I loved that smart girl.

***

Now it was time for something that we all were
dragging on: going back to school. But surprisingly,
nothing popped off. Aryanna was still on me but not
as much as she used to. Maybe she had a change of heart and
felt no interest in me anymore, but that didn't matter. I was
more focused on my schoolwork, cheerleading because we
were in the playoffs, and the teen songwriting competition,
which was due today.

"I can't do it," I told my friends and boyfriend. We all
gathered in my living room just so they could see me submit
and we could celebrate by getting some pizza.

"No, no, no," JaQuan said to me. "You're not going to
back out of this. Now we all read your work, and it is fire."

Not going to lie, it was. But what if the judges over the
contest thought it wasn't?

"Can I read it one more time at least?"

"Girl, you said that four times already," Lauren
complained.

"Nawl, hold on, baby," said Blue. "Let her read it one
more time to clear her head."

My eyes told him *'Thank you so much'*. I read it one
more time. The song is titled *I'm Meant To Be Here.*

I'm not big yet, but I will get there one day,
As long I know that the Lord will never lead me astray,
I know my blessings will come my way,
Letting y'all haters know that I'm here to stay.
I just want to grab my bags and flee,
I wanted peace, so I got on my knees,
Then He came and said, 'I got your future, but you got
the key,'
All the haters are doing is promoting me for free,
But I'm not promoting any beef unless you pay me.

I've been through too much hurt, heartache, and pain,
But my pain will be my gain (repeat 3x).

Why are you trying to stop me from doing me?
This is a part of God's plan, so it's meant to be,
I'm not no wannabe,
You gotta pay my fee,
This is a part God's plan, so it's meant to be.

I felt like this should be good. But I didn't know if it was perfect for it to be a song.

"OK. I think I'm good."

I'm about to submit. I can't. It's just the what ifs.

"Hey," I heard a soft voice behind me. I turned, and it was Ty.

"Let's do it together."

I nodded. We both grabbed the mouse and moved it to the submit button, and we pressed it at the same time.

Congratulations! You have submitted your application and your work. Be on the lookout for an email. Good luck!

"You did it!" Kay-Kay said as she hugged me, and everyone followed suit.

"Now, let's get some pizza!" Jake cheered.

"Man, you are always hungry," Mark joked.

"You look like you need some meat on your bones."

Ty just busted out laughing. Everyone was headed out as Mark and Jake were still roasting each other. JaQuan turned back around to give me some kisses. Once he was done, he looked at me and said, "I'm proud of you."

I smiled, holding back my tears. "Thank you for being there for me."

"Always."

***

This was going to be a very busy week for all of us. The basketball team was in the state championship, so we had cheer practice, practice with the student sections to teach them cheers and chants, schoolwork, and the email that would reveal the top 50 contestants in the songwriting competition went out today.

I decided to skip lunch because I was so nervous about the result. I was walking in the hallway in a circle because of how nervous I was. I was on my phone trying to refresh my email when I felt a bump that dropped my phone. I looked, and it was who it always was.

"You know you should look up from your phone. You'll probably knock someone down." Aryanna winked as Rayanna and Katrina laughed and walked away. D-Rod was behind them, and he walked up to me and asked, "Your phone straight?"

I picked it up, and it was not cracked or anything. I turned to him and nodded.

"Rod!" Aryanna yelled as they were waiting on him.

D-Rod looked at me and wanted to say something, but he walked with him. Besides him constantly wanting to talk to me, he was a good guy. He got along with everyone, had good manners, and seemed like a sweet soul. How did he end up hanging out with Aryanna and started working with her?

I was on the way to cheer/pep squad practice, and I saw D-Rod outside by the back door, and he made a deal with someone. I couldn't deal with it. I went to him, and he was surprised to see me walking up to him.

"Hey, Miss Starr, what can I do for you?" he asked.

"Why are you doing this?" I went straight to the point.

He chuckled. "Do what?"

"Look, I grew up in South Central before I came here. I'm not stupid. You're out here selling candy and leaves."

He looked at me shocked and seemed speechless.

"Look, I've seen how this plays out multiple times. The guy need some quick easy cash, so he decided to get on the street to sell something, he gets too deep in the game and he—"

"Look, I'm not trying to be deep in the game. I just need the money to help my grandma with the bills. She has been working two jobs and barely making enough."

This information was news to me.

"Plus, no one would be my friend because I got held back, and Aryanna was the first person who would give me a chance. She also hooked me up with this gig since she knew my situation and arranged for Rayanna to do my homework."

"Look, if money is what you want, we can help find a job for you that works with your school hours, and we can help you with your homework. This shouldn't be a way for you."

"I appreciate you trying to help me, but I'm way beyond needing help."

"What do you mean?"

He took a quick look around to make sure nobody was around.

"I can't read for real."

I was lost for words. That explained why he was held back.

"Listen, Amber is an avid reader. She'll help you, and I'll make sure this stays between us."

"You sure?"

"I'm positive. Matter of fact, come on."

"Come on where?"

"We're gonna find you some friends. Follow me."

D-Rod shook his head.

"I don't know about this, Starr. What if Aryanna or her crew see me with you?"

He was right. It would cause more tension and more problems.

"Yeah, you're right. I'm not trying to cause trouble. But if you change your mind, we'll be in the gym until 5:30."

He nodded his head, and I went to the gym.

"There you are, Starr," Ms. Kennedy said. "We were wondering where you were."

"I was trying to recruit more people," I replied.

"I see. What's your name, young man?"

Young man?

I heard the gym doors close behind me and turned around. It was D-Rod.

"Destin. Destin Cole."

Mr. Wright was the pep squad's advisor.

Mr. Wright said, "I don't know, Ms. Kennedy. Wildcat Squad, what you think? Should we let Destin join?"

I was expecting them to say no because of who he was hanging out with. But, surprisingly, everyone said yes.

"There's your answer, Ms. Kennedy."

"OK, Destin Cole, go join. The more the merrier."

He seemed hesitant but Ty, who was the pep squad captain, cheered for him.

"Let's go, D-Rod! You have a lot to learn."

Everyone cheered him on, which led him to join the squad in the bleachers.

I quickly ran up to Kay-Kay.

"Hey, we have to help D-Rod on something. I'll tell you later."

Ms. Kennedy then yelled out, "OK, ladies. Let's get into position so that Destin can learn before Friday."

***

"Defense! Defense! Defense!"

This was it. With fifty seconds left, the Wildcats were about to be state basketball champions. The cheerleaders, the fans, and the Pep Squad were celebrating early. We just started dancing and yelled out our chants. Once the buzzer went off, we beat the Hayden Tigers 103-92. This was the school's first basketball championship, and it was exciting to witness history with all

146

my friends. D-Rod seemed to be having the time of his life with Ty, Mark, TJ, and Jake. They were still a little bit suspicious of him, but they were starting to like him. Let's just say that Aryanna wasn't too happy about D-Rod but he ensure me that she'll be alright.

After the boys received their state trophy, they rushed to the hype Avondale crowd. JaQuan won MVP, as he should. We all headed to the bus, and I was looking at the notifications on my phone, and I saw an email that said *Top 50 is moving on!* I opened the email so quickly, searching for my name on the list.

28. Starr Brown- Birmingham, AL.

I couldn't believe my eyes. I had re-read it, I know, at least ten times.

I looked around to find someone to tell this to and I saw Ty. I ran up to him before he got on the bus. Ty looked concerned by the way I came up to him. "What? What? What happened?"

I didn't say anything, I just showed him the email. After he read my email, he gave me a big bear hug.

"I told you! I told you, you could do it!" Ty said.

"I just made the top 50, I probably won't make the next round."

"Look, you are going to the next round. Matter of fact, you'll be the winner of the contest. We are going to claim it and manifest it."

"I hope so. I need to tell JaQuan and the rest of the squad."

"Well, the basketball team left already, and there's an afterparty for them, and almost everyone is going. You want to come?"

Afterparty=a whole bunch of people. No thanks

"Wish I could, but not tonight."

"Alright, that's fine."

"Awwwww, look at that." I rolled my eyes when I heard that voice. "Dang, Starr, you got a man and a side dude, too?" She walked passed me and gave my shoulder a bump.

"Why do you keep messing with this girl, Aryanna?" Ty confronted her.

Aryanna stopped and laughed. "What are you? Her bodyguard?"

"No, but I'm tired of you being a bully."

"How can I bully her? All she has to do is say something to me. Ain't that right, Starr?"

Say something to her. Prove her wrong.

But, I just stood there, not saying anything.

"See, what'd I say?" Aryanna walked off.

Ty turned to me. "Why didn't you say anything? Better yet, why haven't you told anyone that you are her target?"

I sighed. "Because she would make my life hell by speaking out on her, or she will turn the school against me."

"Why do you say that?"

"Because she—never mind. Don't worry about it. Nothing I can do anyways."

Ty shook his head. "Yes, you can. If someone comes forward, it would cause other people to come forward. But somebody has to make that first step."

He was right. Someone had to speak up, but it would not be me.

"Hey, Starr, we gotta go." One of the cheerleaders came up to me.

I nodded at her, and I gave Ty a hug.

"Starr, you can change the culture at Avondale. But you have to change within yourself."

"OK, Ty. I'm glad that you are my friend."

"And I'm glad you are my friend." We said our goodbyes and went to our buses.

It was the day after the game, and I sent everyone a screenshot of the email. Everyone was calling and sending me congratulation texts except JaQuan. Matter of fact, I hadn't heard from him all weekend. I'd tried calling him and texting him, but no response. I was thinking about calling Mrs. Watts to see what was going on until I got a text notification. It was JaQuan.

Can we talk?
I didn't like that.
Yeah. Is everything OK?
Meet me at the park by my house.

***

I was sitting on the swing when JaQuan finally came and sat on the swing next to me.
"Hey," I greeted.
"Hey," he replied.
"So, what do you want to talk about?"
JaQuan let out a huge sigh. "Starr, there's no easy way to say this, but I'm not feeling this anymore."
I was dumbfounded.
"Feeling what?"
"This. Us."
I still wasn't comprehending.
"A-Are you breaking up with me?"
He nodded his head.
Don't cry, don't cry, don't—too late.
The tears were forming.
"W-W-Why? What did I do?"
"I'm just not feeling you anymore, Starr. You're a good person, but you're just not for me."
I started crying. Then something clicked.
"How can I be so stupid?"
"Stupid, how?"
"I fell for the joke that you and Aryanna have on me."
"I don't know what you're talking about."

"Yes, you do. No wonder you guys are still friends. You pretend to like me to get to me and go back to her and talk about me."

"No, no, no, Starr. That's not it."

"Then, what is it? Why are you breaking up with me?"

The silence that he gave me told me everything I needed to know.

"Thought so. You know, I thought you would be different than the people in California. But no, you're no different than them. You two deserve each other." I started walking back home. He tried to call my name, but I ignored him as I silently cried on the way back home.

***

I had been wailing for hours, and my phone kept ringing for the past five minutes. I figured it was JaQuan trying to talk, but I wasn't having it. Then, I had enough and reached for my phone. It was Lauren. I answered it and immediately heard yelling and screaming.

"Hello?"

"Starr?! You need to come to the 32nd Street Market!" Lauren said in a panicked voice.

"Wha-why?"

"Ty was in an accident."

***

The market is just down the street from my house. I ran to the market from my house. When I made it to the scene, and it was chaos. Both cars were totaled beyond repair, police everywhere, and a crowd was still forming. Almost the whole Avondale was here. Even JaQuan. I found Kay-Kay, Lauren, and the twins and ran up to them and gave them a hug.

"What happened?"

Lauren then explained, "Apparently Ty was driving to get some stuff from the store. As he was leaving, a drunk driver was speeding and hit him straight on."

"Oh, my God." I was about to cry again. "Is he alright?"

"We don't know. One of the boys drove to the hospital and they will give us an update soon. Go be with JaQuan. I know he's hurting and needs you."

"I can't."

"Why not?"

I was hesitant to say this, but they were gonna find out sooner or later.

"He broke up with me today."

"WHAT!" they all yelled.

Amber pulled her hair up like she was about to fight.

"Amber, no," Ashley warned her.

"No, because I want to know why," Amber responded angrily.

"We do, too, but now is not the time."

Kay-Kay's phone rang, and she answered.

"Hello... Hey, Mark...What? Mark, don't say that. Please don't say that!"

We all started panicking, asking her what happened, and she started crying. She dropped the phone, and she yelled out, "He's gone! He's gone!"

All I could see was darkness, and all I remembered was hearing screams in the background.

Chapter Nineteen

It had been a few days since Ty's funeral, and I still felt numb. I didn't remember what happened after I received the news, but from what I heard, I was crying hysterically and was yelling. I could believe it. I was so sick right now over losing Ty. He was the only one who knew about the situation with Aryanna and would encourage me and try to make me feel better. Now, I feel horrible because he told me to tell somebody about how bad the bullying has gotten, but I made him promise not to say anything. I hadn't been hanging out with anyone or leaving the house besides school. I hadn't been talking to anybody, not even Kay-Kay. Then, the breakup with JaQuan didn't help. He tried to reach out to me, but I ignored him like the rest. To be honest, I missed him, and I wanted to be there for him because that was his friend too, but I couldn't be there for him as a friend. It was hard to revert back into a friendship after we had been dating for months.

For the last few days, I was dressing like a bum with hoodies, plain t-shirts, plain jeans, and a messy bun. I didn't want to feel pretty anymore. Then, Aryanna would make me feel ugly. She would still push me around and talk down on me like it was nothing. Even though she knew that I was depressed by Ty's death and JaQuan breaking up with me, she didn't care. She wanted me to suffer.

I was chilling at home in my bed as usual when I heard a knock on my door.

"Starr," my momma said as she opened the door. "I know that you're not in the mood for company, but you got some people here for you."

I expected it to be the girls, but it was the guys walking in. TJ, Mark, and Jake.

I stood up in shock.

"What are you guys doing here?" I asked.

"We came to check in on you," Jake responded.

"Well, I'm still alive," I said, hoping to make them leave.

"We clearly see that, but how are you mentally?"

"I'm fine. Why are you here?"

TJ sat on my bed.

"Listen, we all lost Ty, not just you. But we're not going to let you sit here and rot. We know JaQuan breaking up with you for whatever reason was a mess up, but he seems pretty much like a zombie. He wouldn't talk to anyone, he hasn't been playing basketball with us at the park, and he's not even himself. We think he realizes he made a mistake, and you should talk to him."

I rolled my eyes at TJ.

"Also, we know that Aryanna has been bullying you."

I looked at him shocked because how did they know that?

"How?"

"Ty told us," Mark spoke up. "On the night after the championship."

I wanted to say something to them then Jake spoke up to say, "And made us promise not to say anything and to help protect you. Which is why we decided to be your bodyguard for as long as it takes. At least until Aryanna decides to leave you and the rest of us alone."

I let out a huge breath. *Dang, Ty. You always looked out for me, huh?*

"I love you guys. Really, I do but I don't need any protection."

"Then, what *are* you going to do?" Mark asked.

I didn't have an answer to that.

"Listen, we don't care what you say. Ty made us promise that—"

"Ty is gone!" I shouted. "He's gone. Dead. Nothing is going to change that. I don't need any protection. I didn't have any at my old school, so why would I need them now?"

Jake looked confused. "What do you mean that you didn't g—"

"Just get out. Please."

Jake wanted to open his mouth to protest, but Mark grabbed his arm and shook his head. They all started to head to the door.

Jake took one last look and said, "We'll always be your friends. So, you can't get rid of us." Then, they left.

It was then that I received another DM from the anonymous Facebook page and it said, *How are you? I know losing Ty must be hard for you. Why won't you off yourself so you can be with him?*

I wanted to throw my phone across the room, but I knew I might break it. But I started just knocking stuff off my desk and pulling clothes from my closet. Now, different voices went into my head.

How come you don't talk?

Don't even waste your breath, Antwon.

"You're only going to find out how weird she is. Plus, she is probably too busy being with her grown boyfriend. So, she probably is not interested in young guys.

Don't sit next to her. She doesn't talk, and she will stare at you. She's a weirdo.

Weak little girl.

I could feel my heart beating fast. My hands were twitching, my chest was starting to hurt, and I felt dizzy.

No, no, no, no, not this again.

I'm doing what I can to prevent this oncoming panic attack.

Deep breaths.

Deep breaths.

Wheezing, deep breaths. Wheezing, deep breaths.

I can't stop this.

I thought I could control this.
I can't. I can't.
Yes, you can.
That wasn't my voice.
You got this, Starr.
Ty?
Just breathe.
I did as the voice told me.
Inhale, exhale.
Inhale, exhale.
Inhale, exhale.
I calmed down, backed up to the wall, and slid down to the floor and started bawling.
God, please help me.

Chapter Twenty

"Happy birthday to you, happy birthday to you. Happy birthday to Starr. Happy birthday to you!"

I knew I wasn't tripping when I heard my parents singing that song. It was March 27th, my birthday. My sixteenth birthday to be exact. Any regular girl would be excited for their sixteenth birthday to have a big party, but I wasn't that type of girl. I barely celebrated my birthday because I didn't have anyone to invite to any of my birthday parties. Even though I had friends, I still didn't want a party.

I sat up, and I saw my family holding a birthday cake with a 16-candle lit for me.

"Awww, thank you guys." I smiled and blew the candles out.

"Happy birthday, baby girl," Daddy said.

"I can't believe my first born is sixteen," Momma said. "I remember being on the way to the grocery store when my water broke, and I had to drive to the hospital."

"And she called me from work, screaming through the phone, and I had to leave work to hit 80 on the highway."

I rolled my eyes because I heard this story before.

"But, by the time I reached the hospital, you were getting ready to pop out, and they had to prepare for me to give birth. Thank God your daddy made it in time because I was trying to hold off from pushing so he could be there."

"I found her because I could hear her scream from down the hall."

"But in the end, we ended up having a beautiful baby girl, and she turned out to be a very beautiful, smart, and kind young lady."

I grinned. "Thank you. I'm very lucky to be born with this family."

I mean it, too. They were my only friends at one point and my first best friends. They gave me a kiss on my forehead and left me to get ready for school. After my breakdown, I started praying and reading the Bible to help me heal and be closer to God. I started to clean and rearrange my room, and it made me feel lighter. I decided to fix my hair and learn how to braid, and I could say that I did a good job with my box braids. I started back reading books, started back writing poems, and I was hanging out in the library. Reading was starting to be my therapy. I talked to my friends again, but I still kept my distance because I was still trying to heal myself.

Even though I didn't really celebrate my birthday, I still wanted to dress up for my birthday. I decided to wear a black shirt with the face of Tupac, who was one of my favorite rappers besides K'Won, with a black pleated skirt and my black Converses. I'd been practicing my makeup skills, and I decided to put on some makeup today to show everyone my work. I went downstairs for breakfast, and my sister's eyes popped open when she saw me.

"Wow! You look amazing, Starr."

My parents came from the kitchen, and Momma was in awe, but Daddy had that dad look when he realized that his daughter was growing up.

"You look gorgeous, Starr," Momma said.

"You look pretty, Starr," Daddy said. "But I'm just saying, don't you think that…"

"Leave that girl alone, she dresses like a sixteen-year-old. Come on, Starr, I made your favorite."

I couldn't wait to eat my mom's cinnamon waffles.

***

"Happy Birthday!" someone from the hallway said as I walked with Kay-Kay and Lauren. I forgot that I was wearing a birthday sash, crown, and a birthday pin with money.

"Thank you!"

"He's cute," Lauren whispered to me.

"Girl, you with Blue," I reminded her. Yes, they were finally official.

"No, I meant for you."

My chest tightened up a little bit. I missed JaQuan, but I want to know why he broke up with me. Even though he had been trying to talk to me, I wasn't trying to speak with him right now.

"I'm working on myself before I talk to someone else."

"I know that's right, cousin," Kay-Kay chimed in. "Focus on you so you can pop out as a hot girl."

I laughed at her.

"I'm not trying to do that."

"Why not? You're single, you're popping, and all the guys want to talk to you."

"I just want to know the reason why."

"He's probably not going to, but guys are scared to admit their feelings or something."

She was right about that, but the least he could do for me was to be honest with me.

We went to Mr. Wright's classroom, and everyone was telling me Happy Birthday, and I was thanking them. Then, JaQuan came to the classroom, and he saw my birthday gear. He came up to my desk and said, "Happy Birthday, Starr."

I wasn't going to mean today.

"Thanks," I said kind of dry.

He nodded his head as he headed to his chair. I felt like he wanted to tell me something, but he changed his mind. I heard cackling coming from the hall, and the mood in the classroom changed. In walked Rayanna, Katrina, and, of course, Aryanna. Katrina said something to Aryanna and pointed to me. Aryanna's eyes widened seeing me, and she walked up to my desk.

"Oh, wow, Starr. I didn't think you could be dressed up after looking like a zombie for the past few days."

"Shut up, Aryanna," Kay-Kay said to defend me.

"How about you make me?"

Kay-Kay laughed, that was her way of trying not to do anything.

"Aryanna, you're really asking for it, but I'm not going to entertain you."

"Yeah, like I thought," she said as she went to her desk.

I turned to her, and she was shaking her legs and had a look that would burn a hole in the wall. I couldn't blame her though.

"Good morning, scholars," Mr. Wright said as he walked in.

"Good morning," we all said.

He took a look around the class and his eyes landed on me.

"Well, looks like we got a birthday girl in the house."

I smiled at him, hating that he was giving me the spotlight.

"Happy birthday to you."

"Thank you."

"I just so happen to have a gift for you."

"Really?"

"Yeah. I'm giving you a topic for your presentation next week."

I dropped my mouth in shock in a funny way, and everyone was oohing. I knew that my turn to give a presentation was coming, but I still wasn't ready to go up in front of people and talk. But, I had no choice if I wanted to pass his class.

"That's cold, Mr. Wright," I said to him, "But what's my topic?"

"Your topic is bullying."

Wait, what?

"Now, you know the rules. You can do a slideshow, you can talk about a book based on the topic, or you can read a poem. However you want to do it."

I was panicking on the inside. How could I talk about a topic   that   still   affected   me? I knew that once he gave us a topic, we couldn't go and change it, but it was worth the ask. After class, I went straight to his desk.

"If you are coming to talk your way out of the topic, that's not happening," he said to me.

I smacked my lips. "So, there's no other topics that I can do?"

"Nope. What I give is what you'll do."

I said my thanks to him and walked out the classroom.

***

I put that presentation in the back of my mind. I was just trying to enjoy my birthday as much as I could, but I couldn't help but think about Ty and how he would be making this day special for me. Finally, school ended, and I was so ready to go home and have my annual birthday cake and ice cream with my family. I was at my locker, and I heard a voice behind me.

"Hey, Starr." I turned, and it was JaQuan.

He looked handsome as always, but I couldn't give in, so I turned back to unlock my locker.

"Hey, I know we haven't talked, especially after everything that was going on, but I have to tell you something."

"So, now you want to talk?" I turned and snapped at him. "You should've talked to me when you decided to break up with me."

"Listen, I can explain everything. I just want to talk to you."

"OK." I slammed my locker closed. "Talk."

He took a deep breath. "OK, you remember the night of the championship game?"

I nodded my head.

"OK, so we went to the after party, and we had fun. Then, Aryanna was there, and we were hanging out with her. She gave me some juice, and next thing I know, I woke up, and I was at my homeboy's house."

I shrugged my shoulders. "So, what? You got drunk and passed out. What's that have anything to do with it?"

"That's the thing. I didn't drink. I don't drink. I know that I didn't drink any alcohol. But the next morning, I received a text from Aryanna, and it was some pictures of me looking like I was passed out with plastic cups around me and one in my hand. She then said if I didn't break up with you that she would send it around the school to my coaches, to my parents, and to the Anonymous Facebook page so it can ruin my chance to get into any college basketball program."

I couldn't believe what I was hearing right now, but I refused to believe it.

"Here, I'll show you." He pulled out his phone and showed me the messages and the picture. If an outside person saw this, this would be bad because he truly looked like a drunken person that passed out.

"You sure you didn't have a drink before Aryanna gave you one?" I asked to be sure.

"I swear to God that I have never drank alcohol before in my life. You can ask my friends and my teammates. I'm telling you she put something in my drink that made me pass out, and she is trying to do the same thing to you."

I stopped to turn back to him. "What do you mean she is trying to do the same thing with me?" I asked.

"She is plotting to get D-Rod to invite you to a party She is planning on having and trying to pretend to be friendly to you. But she'll try to drug you to put you in a bed and make D-Rod lay there with you to make it seem like you guys had sex together. Then, she would take a picture and post it on Facebook and make it seem like you're easy."

I was stunned. I knew she could go low, but not this low.

"How did you know?" I asked for verification.

"Because D-Rod sent this to me."

JaQuan started playing a video, which was dark, but you could still hear.

"So, you're going to put that in her drink, and she'll be passed out?" That's D-Rod's voice.

"Yep, and I'll put her on the bed, and all you have to do is lay there for a couple of seconds for some pictures." That was Aryanna's voice.

"For what? What are you about to do?"

"Just post some pictures of Starr letting everyone know that she's available for everyone."

"But why? She hasn't done anything to deserve this. She's cool and sweet."

"Please tell me she didn't get to you, too. What is so special about that girl? She's a weak, scary, weird freak that needs to be knocked down a peg or two."

"But, you're going to ruin a girl's reputation for what? What if this leads her to take her own life?"

"I don't care. It'll probably be best for her to go ahead and do it."

I couldn't listen anymore. I couldn't listen to that. I just started running. JaQuan called for me, but I ignored him. I didn't know where I was going, but I had to get out there. I just ran into the restroom to one of the stalls and just started to break down crying.

Why were people so cruel and evil? I didn't do anything to anyone. All I ever did was exist. I didn't deserve this. I couldn't take this anymore.

I started breathing hard, screaming, and crying harder. And harder, and harder.

Then, something just snapped in me.

I'm done.

I went out of the stall to clean up my face, and I exited the restroom. The first thing I went to get were my sweats that I kept in my locker, just in case I had to change. I changed clothes in the restroom and called Kay-Kay.

"Hello?" she answered.

"Kay-Kay," I said. "Do you happen to know where Aryanna would hang out after school?"

"Yeah. Why?"

"Because I want to fight her."

Chapter Twenty-One

"No, Starr," Lauren said as she was walking with me. "Let's just think about it."

"There's nothing to talk about," I told her. I walked out of the school looking for Aryanna, and all my friends were right behind me. There was no changing my mind on this. I was going to fight her. I didn't care if we were gonna fight every day, this had to stop.

"Let her fight, Lauren. If anyone has any reasons to put her down, it's Starr," Kay-Kay said, backing me up.

"Starr, are you sure you want to do this?" Ashley asked me.

"Yeah, she will fight dirty," Amber chimed in.

"Then, we'll have to play in the dirt then," I told them.

A crowd was forming behind me because Blu told a couple of students that I was going to fight Aryanna. I didn't care for the audience, but most of them wanted to see someone beat Aryanna up, so I'd give them a show.

JaQuan saw me walking and the crowd behind me. He looked confused.

"Dude, you need to see this," Jake told him.

"Why? What's going on?"

"Man, your girl about to fight Aryanna," Blue said.

"Wait, what?

"Yeah. It's about to go down."

He didn't come up to me to try to convince me not do it because he knew why I wanted to fight her. I headed towards the park from down the street, which was a known after-school hangout for Aryanna. As I got close to the park, I spotted Aryanna, D-Rod, Rayanna, and Katrina by Rayanna's car. Without thinking, I just started running towards them.

Once I got up to them, I yelled out, "Aryanna!"

She turned to me, gave me a smirk, and turned back to her friends. That only made me frustrated.

"Aryanna, I know you heard me."

"I know. I'm ignoring you," she said, and her friends, except D-Rod, laughed.

The crowd was trying to encourage me to hit her first. Not yet. Not until I read her down.

"Aryanna, I'm not going to ask if it's true because I know it is. You won't stop until you ruin everyone's life, will you?"

She turned to me and shrugged her shoulders.

"I don't know what your problem is with me, but I had enough. You're a mean, cold-hearted bully, and nobody cares for you. Is that why you hate me? Because everyone loves me and hates you?"

I chuckled. "You said that I wanted to be like you, but the whole time you want to be like me."

Aryanna quickly got up to come to my face, and it got the crowd hype. "I don't want to be like you," she said coldly.

"Well, why are you trying to tear me down? You're miserable and unhappy. That's sad. I feel sorry for you."

"You know nothing about me."

"If you keep this up, you'll have no friends. If you keep this up, you'll end up bitter, mean, and mad at the world. Just like your mom."

After I said that, she swung at me, and I leaned back a bit to duck it.

"OOOOOOOHHHHHH!" was all I heard from the crowd.

"I've told you to not talk about my momma," she said as she took her jacket off.

The swing was all I needed. So, I squared up, and she did the same. Almost everyone had their phones out and started recording in excitement.

"So, wassup? You're trying to fight?" she asked.

I wasn't all talk when I fought. I just wanted my rounds.

She got closer and swung again only to miss again. I swung at her, it connected, and it went down. I won't lie, she got the upper hand when she pulled my hair and tried to kick me down. But I kept punching her and used all my upper body strength to put her on the ground, and I kept punching her.

"GO CRAZY, STARR!" Kay-Kay yelled along with the crowd who was rooting for me.

I didn't want to stop because I kept remembering every hit, every word, and everything that she did to me since I'd come to Avondale.

She then let go of my braids, and I still got a grip of her hair, and I was still punching her. Then I decided to kick her, and that's when JaQuan came in and grabbed me.

"OK, that's enough, Starr," he frantically said as he pulled me off.

She got up and charged towards me. I was trying to escape his grip, but JaQuan got a good grip on me. Aryanna looked horrible. Her hair was messed up, her face was dirty, and her nose was bloody. Everyone had their mouths open about how bad she looked. She was still trying to get to me, but D-Rod wasn't allowing it. At this point, I did what I had to do, and I was done.

"Yeah, talk that mess now!" Kay-Kay said, taunting Aryanna. "You got exactly what you deserve! Now post that on Facebook!"

"Man, let go of me!" Aryanna yelled, but D-Rod put her in Rayanna's car, and she was still yelling.

JaQuan let me go. I grabbed my stuff from Lauren, and I started walking away. He called out to me, but Lauren told him to let me walk away. I just wanted to go home.

Chapter Twenty-Two

I couldn't believe I did that. I beat up Aryanna Black, on my birthday in front of the whole school, practically. I turned my phone off because I didn't want to get notifications about the fight or talk to anyone about it. I was in my room just processing what happened. I didn't feel regret about fighting her, but I didn't mean for her to have a bloody nose, even though I didn't feel bad. I felt happy to step up to her, but it shouldn't end like that. I shouldn't have had to fight to stand up for myself, but it happened, and it was probably some videos of the fight going viral on social media. I couldn't do anything about it. I looked at the time, and it was 4:15 PM. My parents were still at work, Skylar was with her friends, and Sekani was still with my maternal grandmother. I decided to take an hour nap to try to forget everything. For now.

***

"Starr?" I heard a voice as I felt someone rocking me. I opened my eyes, and it was my momma. I rubbed my eyes and asked, "What time is it?"
"It's 7:30."
Dang, I've been asleep for that long?
I quickly sat up and said, "I was supposed to take an hour nap. I guess I was tired."
Momma laughed, "What happened at school today that made you tired?"
I felt a lump in my throat.
Just tell her nothing happened.
Tell her nothing happened.
If you say something, it will only make things worse.

"Starr..."

Ty?

"Starr, you can change the culture at Avondale. But you have to change within yourself."

"Momma, I have to tell you something."

"What is it, baby?"

At that moment, I broke down crying, telling her about Aryanna, how she bullied me, that I had to fight her, and the reason why I fought her.

After I told her, my momma sobbed to my story.

"Starr, why didn't you say anything?" she questioned,

"Because I figured if I told the teachers, they wouldn't help me like the teachers back home."

"But you could've told us."

"I didn't want to involve you guys because if she knew I snitched, she'd make my life worse. But even though I didn't say anything, she did it anyway."

"Did your friends know?"

"They knew that she would tease me, but I didn't tell them the other part because I didn't want them to get in trouble."

"Now, you know, Kay-Kay will have your back and will defend you."

"That's the problem. She will fight her on the spot."

"Oh, just like how you did today?"

"Hey, at least I fought her outside of school and didn't get suspended. If I told her that I was being bullied that morning, she would look for that girl after the first period to fight her and won't care if she gets suspended."

We both chuckled because we knew it would be true.

"Aww, baby, I'm so sorry. I should've seen the signs. I should've been more observant..."

"It's not you, Momma. You're right, I should've told you."

"Well, did you win?"

"Yeah, there's a video floating around, so we can look and see."

Momma checked her phone quickly.

"We'll see it later. Let's go to the backyard, your daddy is here with the cake and ice cream."

"OK."

We went downstairs and headed to the backyard. I pulled back the slide, and I heard, "SURPRISE!!!"

I jumped back, and I realized it was my friends, my family, and almost everyone in our class in our backyard with party decorations. I wanted to cry because I never had a party before, and yet, in less than a year of moving here, I had a lot of friends that became family to me despite my social anxiety. I went and hugged my momma, crying.

"Thank you so much. I love you, guys." I said to her,

"We love you, too. You deserve it," Momma replied. I let go and looked down. I realized I was still in my sweats from earlier.

"Oh, my God, why didn't you tell them to change?" I panicked.

"If I told you to change, you will think something is up."

"Oh, Lord, I got to change really quick." I started going up the stairs.

Momma laughed.

"OK, I'll let them know."

***

I changed to a red cami dress and headed to my party. The backyard party was everything I could ever dream of. Lights were everywhere, the DJ was blasting a banging playlist, and everyone was having fun. My Skylar and Sekani were having a hilarious dance battle with Mark and Jake. A couple of K'Won songs came on, and me and the girls were hype and singing the lyrics.

I decided to take a break and sit next to Mark and drink some juice.

"You OK?" I asked.

"I should be asking you that," Mark responded.

"I'm fine."

I noticed that he was looking at Ashley, who was standing around on her phone, and a slow song came on.

"Why wouldn't you ask her to dance?"

"Because she won't go for a guy like me."

"Yes, she would. Trust me. Just go up there and ask her."

It took him a second, but he nodded and went to her and talked to her. All I heard her saying was sure, and she pulled him to the dance floor. He turned back to me to give me a quiet scream and a thumbs up. I gave him a thumbs up in response. I was so happy for him. I watched all the other couples dancing to *Let me Love You* by Mario. It reminded me of JaQuan and what we used to have. I didn't want to admit it, but I missed him. I missed his hugs, his kisses, his laugh, his voice—

"Hey, Starr."

It was like I could hear him right now.

Wait.

I turned, and it was him. I was lost for words at that moment.

"Hey," I said back.

"Are you OK?"

"I'm good."

"That's good. Are you enjoying the party?"

"Yep."

"That's good. Can we talk real quick?"

"If it is something that makes me want to fight Aryanna again, please tell me tomorrow."

"No. It's nothing like that."

I sighed, got up, and we went to a quiet corner.

JaQuan looked me in my eyes. "Listen, I'm sorry. I should have never broken up with you. The moment I sent that text about us meeting at the park on that day, I instantly regret it. I was so worried about my own future that I took you out of it. I can't see a future without you. I know that's crazy to say, but I'm falling in love with you."

My mouth was open, but I couldn't get a word out.

"I know. I know. It was sudden, but no other girl made me feel the way you have me feeling. Starr, I'm so sorry. I don't expect you to take me back now, but I will earn myself being your boyfriend again. But, right now, I'll be alright to be your friend."

This was a lot to take in. No one had ever poured out their feelings for me. Let alone said that they loved me.

JaQuan said he loves me. THE JaQuan Watts said that he loves me.

I took a moment to process everything, and I made my decision.

"No."

JaQuan looked hurt and on the verge of tears. "I understand. Just hope one day you'll forgive me," he said as he started walking off. I grabbed his arm to pull him back to kiss him on the lips. Once, I pulled back, he had a confused smile on his face that made me laugh.

"I was saying no because I don't want to be just friends. I want to be more than that. JaQuan, before I got here, I couldn't talk to a guy like you or make friends. I was so quiet, and I couldn't talk to the other kids because of my anxiety. Then, the kids started bullying me from kindergarten to ninth grade because of it. It got so bad that I had to beat up a girl and got suspended and basically turned everyone against me, including someone that I thought was my friend. That's the main reason that we moved here. We came so I could start over. That's why I held on to the bullying for so long until I exploded today. Because I don't want to get in trouble and have the whole school turned against me. Now, I realize that I have family, friends, and a boyfriend that have my back. No matter what."

JaQuan hugged me and gave me a peck on my forehead.

"Thank you for telling me your story. I wish you would've told me about Aryanna. I would've stood by you. I know she can be a bit mean, especially with her past, but I never thought she would go this far."

"You would have believed me?"

"Of course, because I knew you wouldn't make something like that up."

"That's good to know that."

"Sooooo, this means we're back together?"

"I mean, we could be just friends or whatever—"

"No. I'm good as your boyfriend."

"Good." I gave him another kiss.

We walked back to the party to enjoy the rest of the night.

Chapter Twenty-Three

It was the next morning, and me, my friends, and JaQuan were hanging out in the park.

"Boy, we had a good time last night," TJ said to us.

"Yeah, we did a good job." Lauren said.

"Well, the guys did most of the work. Y'all were bossing us around," Blue chimed in to throw shade at Lauren.

"Well, either way, I enjoyed it, and I thank you guys for the party," I said to them,

"You know we love you, Starr," Kay-Kay said.

"Also, I'm sorry I didn't tell you guys about Aryanna. I didn't want you guys to get in trouble."

I ended up telling them that the reason why Aryanna went after them was because of me. They surprisingly took the news well because they knew that it wasn't my fault.

"Starr, quit apologizing. We forgive you," Jake chuckled.

"Yeah, but I still feel bad."

"Starr, the great Kevin Hart once said, 'The day you sign up to be best friends, that means that our mess is your mess, and your mess is our mess.'"

We're going to have your back no matter what, and if we get in trouble for it, then they're going to have to suspend me. Because I will fight to defend y'all to the end."

"You got that right," the twins said in unison.

We all laughed.

I looked up at the sky.

"I wish Ty could see us now," I said.

"He is, babe," JaQuan comforted me. "He's always here with us."

"Oh, snap!" Blue shouted. "What up, D-Rod!"

D-Rod was walking towards us, and we saw Rayanna and Katrina walking behind him.

Before I knew it, Kay-Kay got up and yelled, "Uhn-uhn, what are they doing here?"

"They wanted to come, too," D-Rod responded.

"Well, you might as well turn around so they can turn around too."

"Why do I have to leave?"

TJ stepped up in front of Kay-Kay. "Listen, we love you, bruh, but we don't want them around us. They're Aryanna's friends."

Katrina stepped up and said, "Listen, I don't expect y'all to like us, but all we ask is for you guys to listen to us."

"What do you have to say to us?"

"Not you. Starr."

I perked up.

"Nawl, what you got to say to her, you say to us." JaQuan came to my defense.

"It's OK." I stood up. "I got this."

I wanted to show everyone that I wasn't scared anymore. I walked up to them.

"What do you want to talk about?"

"Look," Katrina spoke up. "I know we're the last people that you want to see, but we have to warn you."

"Warn me about what?"

"Aryanna is planning to sneak you."

I wasn't trying to look shocked, but I was thrown off.

"What do you mean?"

"She's planning on attacking you in Mr. Wright's class?"

"WHAT?" my friends yelled.

"Yeah," D-Rod chimed in. "She wants to mess her up."

"Not if I get to her first," Amber told him.

"Well, you're gonna have to get her after me. This is my cousin she is messing with," Kay-Kay fumed.

"Hold on y'all," I told them so they would calm down. I asked, "How do you know this?"

Katrina pulled her phone out to play a video. It was dark, but you could still hear the voices.

"Man, Ary, chill! It's over with!" D'Rod yelled.

"Don't tell me to chill! I need my lick back!"

"Ary, let it go. Y'all fought, and you lost. It is what it is."

"No. I'm not letting this down. She talked about my momma and embarrassed me in front of the school. I'm not letting nothing slide. I'm just gonna have to see her on Monday in Mr. Wright's."

"OK, Ary, it's not that deep," Rayanna expressed.

"Man, Rayanna, shut up before I fight you. Since you want to defend her, let me take my anger out on you."

It was silent for a minute.

"Katrina, you got something to say?"

Another silence.

"That's what I thought. Man, I can't wait to see her on Monday and see if she can still talk that talk when I'm making her bleed on her face."

The video ended, and I got angry all over again.

"OK, let's do it."

"Starr, no," Ashley scolded me.

"No, she just said she'll make me bleed. That's a threat. Now, I want to fight again. Matter of fact, where she at? I want to fight her now!"

"JaQuan, please come and get your wannabe gangsta girlfriend and calm her down," Kay-Kay told him.

JaQuan held on to me as I was blowing in anger.

"Calm down, Starr," Ashley said in her soft voice and turned to Rayanna and Katrina.

"How are we supposed to know that this isn't a set up? How do we know that y'all are telling the truth?"

"That's a good question," Rayanna responded. "I know we were bullies, too, and we were joking, but we never

175

thought she would go this far and try to harm anyone. I swear on my dead grandma's grave that we want to take her down."

"How?" I questioned.

"We got something on her for you to go to the principal," D-Rod answered that for us.

After he told us what they had on Aryanna, we started plotting.

Chapter Twenty-Four

"You don't have to follow me, guys."

It was Monday, and we were waiting for Aryanna to come so the plan could fall into motion. I walked through the hallway, and I had my "bodyguards" with me, AKA TJ, JaQuan, and Jake.

"Listen, we are here to make sure she doesn't attack you," JaQuan told me.

"Or you attack her," TJ added.

I rolled my eyes. "I'm not going to attack her."

"Man, please. You were ready to demolish that girl."

"OK, maybe I was, but I'm not going to today."

"Mhmmmm…"

We made it to my locker, and Mark jogged passed us to tell us, "She's coming."

The guys assumed the position.

OMG, she's coming.

Breathe, Starr, and follow the plan.

I was pretending to get stuff from the locker.

"What's going on, Ary?" JaQuan faked his greeting. Next thing I heard was someone struggling trying to get through. I turned around, and it was Aryanna trying to get to me, but TJ and JaQuan held her back. Then, Jake got in front of me.

"Let me go!" she yelled out.

"Naw, bruh. You're tripping," JaQuan told her.

"Aryanna, I'm not trying to fight you," said in my fake innocent voice.

"Oh, but I am."

"What did I do to you?" I started fake crying, "Just leave me alone."

"Oh, now you want to start crying? You'll be crying for real when I get done with you." She was still trying to get to me when we heard, "Hey! What's going on?" Mr. Wright yelled out in the hallway.

"Black! What are you doing?"

She wasn't saying anything. She got loose and tried to get to me, but Mr. Wright grabbed her and pulled her away through the now formed crowd.

"Let me go, I still want my ones with her! LET ME GO!"

"Aryanna, head to the office!"

I grabbed my bookbag and started heading to the office. I pretend to wipe my tear walked past Rayanna who was "recording" on Aryanna's phone. We gave each other a quick smirk, and I left.

***

"OK, Ms. Brown," Mr. Phillip, the principal said as he sat down and grabbed his pen and paper. "Now, let's talk about what happened…"

"Where should I start?" I questioned.

"Let's start from what led up to today."

"How far do you want me to go?"

"Let's start from the beginning."

For the next two and a half hours, I told him everything that Aryanna Black had done to me and my friends from the first day of school till now. I couldn't help but to say that I felt a huge weight lifted from my shoulders. Reliving those moments was bringing me to tears, but I couldn't show it.

As I was answering his questions, there was a knock on the door. It opened and revealed Mr. Wright.

"Mr. Phillips, may I see you out here?"

"Excuse me, Ms. Brown."

I nodded. They left the door barely open, and I heard them talking about a phone and Facebook, and I knew then, they got the phone. The plan was to convince Aryanna to let Rayanna record the fight and post it on the Anonymous Page to embarrass me. But the plan was to have Aryanna login in on the app and show that it was her who was behind the page and made all those posts. From what D-Rod had told me, Mr. Phillip had been getting reports about the post and getting complaints from parents ever since the page was created. Different students went to Mr. Phillip to tell him that they thought it was Aryanna. He brought her in for questioning, but because of the fact that there was no proof that it was her, he let her go. But now, he finally got the proof that he needed.

Mr. Phillip came back in and asked me, "So, umm, Ms. Brown, anything else you want to say?"

"Umm, did you find the brass knuckle?" I asked.

"What brass knuckle?"

"She has this brass knuckles, and she uses it to threaten other students and would carry it around in her bookbag."

Thanks for that fact, Katrina.

"OK, thank you for telling me that. Is there anything else you want to say?"

I shook my head.

"Alright, we will be taking this matter very seriously and will be looking into it. Ms. Brown, thank you so much for coming in and talking to me."

"Thank you for taking the time to listen to me."

I was leaving the main office when I got a notification from my phone.

Bae 😊 *: Check your Facebook.*

I opened up my Facebook, and the first thing I saw was someone sharing a video from a blank Facebook page, and it had a secret recording of Aryanna admitting that she was the one behind the Avondale Anonymous Page. The reactions and the backlash were insane. People were making fun of her, others wanted to fight her, and others were putting their two cents in. This was getting insane. I felt bad, but I didn't feel bad. Even though I never intended for things to go this far, we had to do something to make the bullying stop, and I didn't care how people looked at me. If I was the bad person for speaking out, then lock me up and throw away the keys. From this point on, I was going to stand up for myself and others.

I was walking in the hallway to go to my locker, and I turned the corner. I saw JaQuan leaning his back against my locker. I walked up to him, and I broke down bawling as we embraced each other.

He whispered, "Starr, you are an amazing person. You have overcome so much. When you came to Avondale, you were a closed clam, and now, you opened up to be a beautiful pearl. You've shown that you are bigger than your anxiety and that you can overcome anything. I'm so proud you."

I let go to wipe my tears.

"Thank you. Thank you for being everything I ever wanted in a friend and more. You are an amazing guy. I never thought I would find a person like you in my lifetime. I love you."

"I love you, too."

I gave him a few pecks as the bell rang.

"Want me to walk you to class?" he asked me.

"Yes, you can," I responded.

***

It was Friday, and through the week, it had been peaceful. I hadn't seen or heard anything from Aryanna all week, and I was relieved. Even though I knew she was probably coming back soon, but I was ready for whatever.

"Starr!" Mark yelled across the hall as I was heading to Mr. Wright's class. I rolled my eyes. *What now?*

"First off, I got good news, and mind-blowing news."

"What's the good news?" I asked.

"I followed your advice, and I asked Ashley on a date. She said yes!"

I gasped and happily gave him a hug.

"That's great, Mark. I'm so happy for you!"

"Yes, but now I need help setting this date up."

"Sure, we got you. Now, what's the mind-blowing news?"

"Word going around school is that Aryanna got expelled."

Shocked wasn't the word close enough to how I felt.

"Are you serious?"

"Yeah, it was crazy, it happened just now."

Then, I immediately thought about D-Rod. What if she told them that he was selling, too? I left Mark and speed-walked to find him at his locker.

"D-Rod," I panicked.

D-Rod turned to me, looking concerned.

"What's going on, Starr?"

"Have you heard about Aryanna?"

"Yeah, I heard."

I started panicking even more.

"Oh, my God, what if she tells on you? What if you get in trouble? I don't want you to get in trouble."

"Girl, calm down."

"No! She might get you in trouble. Then you will be expelled. I would feel so bad that she—"

"They're not going to come to me."

Now I was confused.

"What do you mean?"

He explained that Rayanna went through their messages and permanently deleted them before she gave Mr. Phillip the phone. Then, he told me that he no longer carried or sold drugs after we convinced him to stop.

I let out a sigh of relief. He laughed at me.

"Did you really think I was that stupid to still have some drugs on me?"

"No, I just got worried for a second."

"Starr, I'm fine. I'm good. Now, go to class before you be late."

I just smiled and headed to class.

***

"Starr, it's time for your presentation."

As nervous as I was now, I was so ready to share my poem with the class.

I got to the front, and I was about to read when Mr. Wright interrupted me saying, "Hold on, before you say anything, I have something to say. Starr, thank you."

OK, I'm confused.

"Now I know you're confused, but I want to say thank you for your presentation on Monday."

Monday?

Mr. Wright turned to the class.

"Everyone, on Monday, Starr did something that not many people will do. She decided to take a stand against bullying, and I was there to witness it. For the past few months, I have witnessed this girl suffering in silence, and I had done everything I could from behind the scenes to try to find help for her, but I heard from different people that if she didn't speak up about it, that there was nothing that they could do. But may I say, this is one brave girl, and I applaud her for that."

Mr. Wright started clapping, and the rest of the class followed behind him. JaQuan then stood up, still clapping, and everyone else stood up along with him. I couldn't hold back the tears. I put my hand on my heart because I FELT overwhelmed. Looking at my friends and my classmates made me happy because they were standing beside me.

After they got done clapping, I responded by saying, "Thank you guys so much."

"Now, with that being said, you don't have to read anything. So, you can go ahead and take a seat."

I was really hesitant to sit down. I turned to him.

"Would it be alright if I go ahead and read this poem?"

Mr. Wright popped his eyes open.

"This is the first time that I let a presentation slide, and you still want to do it?"

"Yes."

"Well, you have my blessings."

I cleared my throat and started reading,

There was once a Broken Girl
Her life was in spiraling swirl,
All she wanted to be was a good schoolgirl,
But they made fun of her curls,
She was surrounded by mean girls,
She had no friends to play,
Took her money, with no lunch to pay,
They all thought she might be gay,
They were lions, and they all looked at her as prey,
She got on her knees to pray,
For everything to go away.
Make it go away!
Make it go away!
Make it go away!
I don't care if I have to die, just make it go away!
Then, something clicked, and she look in the mirror and
saw a pearl,
She was proud of her nappy curls,
She was going to stand up against those mean girls,
She would find some real homegirls,
She would continue to be a good school girl,
She would no longer be a Broken Girl,
She will and would be that Girl.

After I got done, the class erupted in claps and whoops. I felt so overwhelmed with the responses.

I was walking to my seat when JaQuan came to give me a hug, and my friends came to give me a big group hug. For the first time in my life, I could finally breathe.

Epilogue

Three months later...

"Right this way, Ms. Brown," Mrs. Collen, the rep for *Black Teen Magazine,* said as she took me to a studio session. Yes, I was in the top five winners for the songwriting contest, and I was in Atlanta for my first day of my internship.

The last few months had been a roller coaster. After what was discovered in Aryanna's locker and after multiple people that came forward to report her bullying, she was expelled and was sent to an alternative school. Even though she got what she deserved, I still hated to see her go through that. I felt sorry for her, and I hoped one day she'd learn her lesson and get some help. But I wished nothing but the best for her.

But, everyone was doing great. JaQuan and I were still going strong. He was currently playing in an AAU team back at home. Lauren and Blue were still together and were literally couples' goals. Mark and Ashley were still dating. Amber was still single, but we're trying to find someone for her, but she was too focused on junior year. Kay-Kay was still Ka-Kay, and TJ asked for my help to try and set up a date with her. Jake was doing great, and he kept track of me as if he was my big brother. But I loved him for that. Rayanna and Katrina were good, I guess. I hadn't talked to them much since that Aryanna situation. D-Rod was doing great. He got a job as a cashier at a local grocery store and his reading ability improved tremendously, thanks to everyone pitching in to help him. Especially Amber, who I think was feeling him, but you didn't hear that from me. But I would forever love my friends.

"You ready?" Mrs. Collen asked me when we reached the door of the studio.

"As ready as I will ever be."

We walked into blasting sounds and a group of people standing around. We made our way through the mini crowd just to be shocked about who was jamming to the beat and reading my lyrics out loud.

"Starr, meet K'Won. K'Won, this is Starr. The wonderful writer behind your song."

K'Won turned around and gave me a smile.

"Wassup, my name is K'Won."

AHHHHHHHHHHHHHHHHHHHHHHHHHHHHHHHHHHH HH!

Be cool. Be cool. Be cool.

"Hi, I'm Starr."

"Starr, may I say that your lyrics are fire, and I can't wait to record it."

"I can't wait to hear it."

"So, what made you write it? What inspired you to write that?"

I shrugged my shoulders.

"Just the story of my life."

"Yeah, I can relate to the song. That's why I picked it because it reminds me of being at my old house back in Zone 6, and I fantasized about being famous and moving my momma and grandma out of the hood. Now, look at me."

"Yep. The top teen rapper in the industry. May I say, I'm a huge fan, and I feel so blessed that you picked my song."

"Thank you so much for your support. I feel blessed by picking this song. I hope this will reach all the hood babies in the world."

"Ayo, 'Won, time to hit the booth," one of the producers said.

K'Won nodded his head and turned back to me.

"I hope you don't mind me tweaking the lyrics."

"No, it's fine. Do what's best for the song."

"Alright, bet. I hope you enjoy it."

"If it's coming from you, I already know it will be good."

I found a chair to sit in and just savored the moment. I couldn't believe that about a year ago, I was ready to give up on life and on the verge of suicide. Now, I was here with the biggest artist in the world right now, and he was going to rap to my lyrics. God was truly amazing.

***

"Thank you so much." I thanked Mrs. Collen as I left the black Cadillac truck to go to the Georgia State dorm that I was staying in.

"No problem. Be sure to make the 10 PM curfew, and if you want to go somewhere before then, let the lady at the front desk know."

"Yes ma'am. I will."

"Alright, see you tomorrow."

"Alright, bye."

I closed the door, and she and her driver drove off.

My phone started to ring. It was JaQuan.

"Hello?" I answered.

"What's good?"

"Nothing much, just heading back to the dorm."

"Oh OK. How was your first day?"

"It was amazing. You won't believe who I met today."

"Really? Who?"

"You know I can't say."

"Why not?"

"Because I'm not supposed to say."

"You know you can tell me. I won't say anything to the crew."

I laughed as I entered the building.

"I know I can tell you. But I can't say it over the phone."

"Then, how about in person?"

I was thrown off until I turned the corner and saw JaQuan walking up and holding flowers. I dropped my stuff to run to him and jump on him.

I kissed him as I got down and I asked, "What are you doing here? How did you get here?"

"My dad had a conference, and I'm off this week, so I tagged along," he explained.

"So, you'll be here for a week?" I squealed.

He nodded his head and hugged him again.

"What do you want to do first?" I asked.

"You hungry?"

"Very."

"We can go to the Metro Diner. It's close by, and I have my car."

"OK. I'll meet you outside. I have to let them know that I'm about to leave."

"OK."

I picked my stuff up from the ground and let the front desk ladies know that I was leaving for a while. I went outside when he pulled up to the front. I got inside and gave him a quick peck.

As he pulled off, he asked me, "So, who did you meet that made you so excited?"

I smiled at him. I couldn't wait to tell him that I met my favorite rapper and that I'd be writing more of his songs on his next album. I was looking forward to leaving the past behind me and seeing what the future had in store for us.

THE END

ABOUT THE AUTHOR

Kiki Ellyse was born in Birmingham, AL but was raised in Fairfield, AL. She has always had a creative mindset ever since she was young. She loves reading books and would carry books wherever she went. She started writing short stories in elementary school and developed the passion to write books. She is a proud graduate of Fairfield High Preparatory School. She is also a proud graduate of Miles College, an HBCU, where she earned her Bachelor of Science degree in Business Administration in three years. Now, she is currently a Library Assistant, hoping to be a Librarian one day. When she's not writing, she loves watching movies, especially horror movies, loves to travel, and watching documentaries that are based on Black culture.

Social Media

Follow me for updates and new releases:

Author Kiki Ellyse

@author_kikiellyse

Made in the USA
Columbia, SC
01 October 2024

42637633R00113